Expressions of the Eternal

Swami Purnamritananda Puri

Mata Amritanandamayi Center
San Ramon, California, USA

Expressions of the Eternal
By Swami Purnamritananda Puri

Published By:
Mata Amritanandamayi Center
P.O. Box 613, San Ramon, CA 94583-0613 USA

In India:
www.amritapuri.org
inform@amritapuri.org

In Europe:
www.amma-europe.org

In US:
www.amma.org

INTRODUCTION

Om Amriteswaryai Namah

At that sacred point of silent stillness, where all the worlds and time meet, the Divine Mother's deepest compassion pours as ambrosial showers. Her motherly love seeps into our troubled minds like a stream of cool, nurturing water, evoking tender memories in our inmost being.

Through the language of love, Amma demonstrates how worship is the means to awaken and know the all-pervading invisible power in our own Self. That power is like the music hidden in the keys of the piano.

Mother smiling through tearful eyes; children struggling to hold back tears—this was the scene that unfolded one *Onam* evening, against the background score of sea waves. Amma then revealed the great truth that all—both the sentient and the insentient—are Her children. This book also shares the blessing of being able to bear witness to the momentous occasion when the Avatar revealed the secret of Her Incarnation.

Experiences revealing the power of pure faith and divine love are common occurrences in Amma's presence. Just as all the water in a large tank is available through a tap, observing Amma, we see how the small body of a *mahatma* (spiritually illumined soul) can manifest infinite divine power. All who have taken refuge in Her arms will have a thousand memories, like precious gems. I have shared just a few of my experiences here.

Using the simplest language, Amma conveys how we can make our lives meaningful. She understands the poor man's life, and his desires, heartaches and struggles. She wipes away

his tears, and uplifts him. The golden rays of Her love spread rainbows of hope and bliss in Her children's tear-soaked eyes. Like Lord Sri Krishna, who blessed Kuchela with both worldly and spiritual wealth, Amma leads us from the sorrows of worldly life to the eternal bliss of immortality.

She imparts the knowledge by which we can rid ourselves of fear here and now, and become embodiments of love and immortality. She tugs the boats of life tossing about in the ocean of transmigration to the safe shores of peace. Let us pray to this embodiment of love that transcends space and time to lead us, too, to that shore of bliss.

Om Namah Sivaya!

Contents

1

Decoding the Drama of Divine Descent

It might seem like a story—not the story of one who might have lived, but that of one who came back to life from death. After all, don't most people in this world live like they are dead?

Distraught souls wander hither and thither, reaching out to this and that in the pursuit of happiness! They speed along, caught in the torrent of endless desires. They are borne helplessly by the tide of life, not knowing where they are headed. Little do they realise that they will soon end up in the abysmal depths of the ocean!

It is best not to be carried away by the colourful pageant of the world's manifold pleasures, which are transient. Yet can we stand apart from the vagaries of creation? Grace alone can save us from the whirlpools that can trap even the most adept. These deadly whirlpools lurk even where the water seems most placid. The only solution is to heed the counsel of those who have experienced it all, the wise ones who often do not get the chance to tell others of it. The great actor who knows the secrets of the drama of life returns. The director, producer and actor are all one and the same person! He alone makes us sing the songs of love and melodies of grief. All these may be found in the movie of life. But what if we considered them real? That is where inner conflict arises. Life then becomes a great battle. Nature's repository of benevolence is transformed into an armoury of lethal weapons. Rivers of blood flow. Everything ends in a woeful wail. However, the *jnani*, the omniscient one, who knows both the players and the playhouse are oneself, sports an unfading beatific smile. If all is one's own Self, there is no other with whom to wage war. What is there to win?

Not many are blessed with the opportunity to witness the divine *lilas* (divine play) of an Avatar, who can transform even *yuddha* (war) into *yajna* (holy sacrifice). Nor do all who are blessed to witness them understand them. Those who attempt to analyse the acts of this divine magician fail. The Dushasanas (a character from the *Mahabharata*) who dare disrobe the goddess, i.e. who try to unveil her secrets, die in the attempt. Even hearts brimming with devotion to the Lord cannot comprehend all His lilas.

Nature cannot disregard the advent of a divine actor, who will teach the secret of transforming yuddha into yajna. Preparations for that advent would have begun much in advance.

Sri Sugunanandan, fortunate to be the father of Amma, once recounted an incident that occurred long before the divine drama of Her life began. A wandering *yogi* arrived at their home and stood with eyes closed. Amma's parents, Sugunachan (as he was called by all of us) and Damayanti-amma, bowed down to him and welcomed him reverentially. Sugunachan did not realise then that the yogi's words were part of the opening scene of the drama of incarnation. His words echoed in Sugunachan's heart for long afterwards: "This is a blessed place. It is about to give birth to a *Maha-guru* (great master), who will hold the entire world in a loving embrace. Many yogis will attain *samadhi* (merger with Infinity) here. It will become a pilgrimage centre in future. This land will come to be known all over the world. I bow to you, who are going to be parents to a great avatar, who, as the very epitome of motherhood, will wipe away the tears of millions of people." They were fortunate enough to see the *yogi's* words come true and witness Amma's Avatar-*lila*.

Though he was strict, Sugunachan had a special fondness for me, and did not hesitate to share some of his experiences with me. He recounted the occasion on which Amma first revealed the secret of Her divine incarnation. As a child, She used to call Sugunachan 'stepfather' whereas She called elderly men as 'father'. The fact that She addressed him alone as stepfather greatly disturbed him. Once, he asked Her why She did so. Amma said, "All parents in this world are merely stepmothers and stepfathers. God alone is our real father and mother. Are parents able to bring a dead child back to life? How, then, can they then claim to be real parents? All are children of God alone. Earthly fathers and mothers are all only stepparents!"

Sugunachan witnessed many wondrous events in Amma's childhood. In Her early years, He never agreed with any of Her views. In fact, he usually held contrary views! But time and experience taught him a lot. The last article he wrote for the *Matruvani* magazine was entitled 'My Daughter, My Mother'. How can one's daughter become one's mother? Yet such is Sugunachan's story. He brought Amma up as his daughter, and then realised She was his Mother, and still later, his Guru.

In the early years, Amma used to be constantly absorbed in *Devi Bhava Samadhi* (absorption in the manifestation of divinity as the Goddess). Sugunachan was not aware of the nature of Amma's divinity. He tried many ways to get his daughter back to 'normalcy'. He tried many tactics to rid Her of Devi, to no avail. Amma simply couldn't heed Her parents' wishes in this matter because Her goal was to fulfil not the *dharma* of a daughter, but that of a World Teacher. For this reason, She could never live Her life on their terms or in accordance with their wishes. As far as they were concerned, people were coming to their home to meet their teenage daughter. The simple villagers that they were, they did not have the necessary spiritual background to fathom the significance of the events unfolding before their eyes. They had faith in temples, but the *gurukula* (ancient Indian education system) culture was alien to them. Slander and accusations began to come their way. Amma's unmarried sisters lived in the same house, and Sugunachan feared that these goings-on would hamper their marriage prospects. Tormented by such thoughts, he became unhappy. His simple understanding was that Amma was possessed by the Divine Mother.

Finally, one night, while Amma was giving Devi Bhava darshan in the *kalari* (small shrine on the premises of the Amritapuri *Ashram*), he entered the shrine and requested Devi, "I want my daughter back. Devi, please manifest elsewhere!"

Amma asked, "Is this body what you mean when you say 'your daughter?'"

"Yes!" he said.

"If so, here she is! Take her!" replied Amma. Hearing this, the devotees became apprehensive about what was going to happen. The crowd became silent. A few moments went by. Presently, Amma's body fell off the *peetham* (elevated seat) on which She had been sitting. There was no breath or pulse. Amma had given away the body that the father considered his daughter, but it had no life in it! People stood shocked. She was dead, in accordance with the norms of medical science. Her body was brought out to the veranda and laid there. A lamp was lit. Amma's heartbroken mother, siblings and other relatives started crying uncontrollably. A few devotees lay their heads on Amma's peetham in the kalari with tearful eyes. All remained praying until daybreak.

A totally distraught Sugunachan fell at Amma's feet. He begged Devi to forgive his ignorance. Hugging Amma's feet tearfully, he prayed, "O Devi! I beg You, forgive me for the words that I uttered in extreme ignorance! Please bring my daughter back to life! Forgive my sin! Never again will I repeat this despicable action!" He prayed fervently.

A long time later, Amma opened Her eyes. The devotees started crying even louder in happiness. Amma's eyes were full of boundless love and compassion. For the first time, She revealed the purpose of Her advent and informed Sugunachan of Her divine purpose and mission on earth. She said, "I was not born to remain confined within the walls of a house all my life. My life is for the world. I have come to save millions. My children will come in search of me from all parts of the world. You should also consider them your children. Do not ask anyone for anything. Whatever is needed will come by itself. Henceforth, your dharma is to serve the devotees. I will remain here if you will obey my words. If not, I will leave this body."

Hearing these words, Sugunachan promised with the utmost reverence and humility, "Please forgive me. My words arose from a father's pain and concern for his daughter. Please forgive my audacity in considering the Goddess my daughter. I understand now. For the rest of my life, I will be happy to serve the world and the devotees who come here."

Following this incident, Amma's home became a refuge for Her devotees. Her family looked after the devotees, offering them food and shelter even when they themselves had to go without food or find shelter elsewhere. They did not complain or retaliate when derided by the ignorant, and faced every difficulty with forbearance. Once, when the ashram was attacked by armed atheists, Sugunachan and Amma's siblings formed a circle around us and protected us from harm, even though themselves they were hurt in the process. They never went back on their promise.

Sugunachan dedicated the rest of his days for the good of the world, thus sanctifying his life. He had gifted the world a daughter capable of shouldering all its sorrows. At last, when the blessed father left his body, he did so with the awareness that his dear daughter was indeed the embodiment of divine love, the great Goddess who was sanctifying and saving the world.

2

Invisible Arms that Embrace

Bharat (ancient name of India) is the hallowed land of great sages, where God incarnates in human form again and again to enact His divine drama. It is the land that teaches its people to pray for the wellbeing of all. Amma always reminds us, "We must constantly bear in mind that the whole world is a single family." We are now busy dividing ourselves in the name of caste, faith, country, language and politics, whereas Amma is striving to unite us all, making the world one family – *Amritakutumbam* (the Amrita family; immortal family life).

In the *Ramayana*, sage Valmiki offers the world Sumitra's message of unity.

Ramam Dasaratham viddhi
Mam viddhi Janakatmajam
Ayodhyam atavim viddhi
Gacha thatha yatha sukham

Lakshmana, about to accompany Sri Rama who is leaving for the forest, seeks blessings from his mother Sumitra. The mother imparts a noble message and blesses her son. It is a message that every mother in the world should impart to her children: "Consider Rama your own father Dasaratha, Sitadevi as your own mother Sumitra, and the dense forest as your kingdom Ayodhya. Go and come in peace, my child!" Sumitra's advice shows that the mothers of Bharat had the strength to impart messages that were potent enough to transform generations.

To consider Rama one's father is to treat and respect all elders as one would one's own father. To consider Sita one's mother is to revere all women as one would one's own mother, irrespective of their age. To consider the dense forest the city of

Ayodhya is to see all the countries of the world as extensions of one's homeland. To do so, one must first learn to love one's own country and culture. By doing so, one can enjoy heavenly bliss even in the most difficult situations.

In Amma's divine presence, we are able to savour Her divine Love. Forgetting their differences, all kinds of people come together as Amma's darling children. This opportunity to have the Divine Mother's *darshan* and to bathe in the sea of Her divine love is the result of the *punya* (spiritual merit) gained in past lives.

Some people ask, "Why does Amma hug people from all over the world?" She has been doing so since Her teens. She sits for hours on end to embrace thousands. In that divine embrace, people feel secure, find solace, and experience true love. They realise that they have found someone who knows them thoroughly. That realisation gives them the strength to go forward in life. The young, the old, the sick, the healthy, the rich, the poor—all receive the same unconditional love from Her. Amma prioritises the needs of others over Her own.

After meeting Amma, I tried to tell my friends about Her. I was a college student then. A classmate asked me what was special about Amma. I said, "She hugs hundreds of people every day with deep love and compassion."

He asked, "What's so great about Amma's hugging? I could do it as well!"

The next day, my friend accompanied me to the ashram for Amma's darshan. He wanted to tell Her that he could do anything She did. However, seeing Amma hug a leper and lick his wounds, he fell unconscious. In an instant, the atheist was miraculously transformed! Never again did he scorn Amma.

The lines that a pious poet penned after witnessing that scene come to mind:

She caressed and comforted him
who was stricken by leprosy,
licking away the pus
that oozed from the mouth of the sores.
She longed to take on all his agonies.
No doubt, She was creating the most
glorious histories of compassion.

Years later, my friend chanced to meet this leper at the ashram again. He was amazed by the story of his healing. When asked what medicine had cured him, his said, "Amma's maternal love! Even my birthmother wasn't able to love me. Who would feel love for this disfigured form with smelly sores all over? It is easy to love those who are good-looking, affluent and highly placed. But who would feel compassion for this lowly one with a contagious disease? Not that I have any complaints. Who to complain to? I didn't come to Amma in the hope of getting cured, only for a drop of love. She gave me the magic potion of Her affection."

Only motherly love can heal the wounds inflicted by worldly life. Humans roam about for want of love. Their hearts break for lack of love. Their souls pine for love. What humans need is love, self-assurance. This self-assurance is what Amma is trying to give through motherly love. What might the mother give her grieving child other than a hug mixed with boundless love and affection? With every hug, Amma also absorbs the burden of our sin.

Amma says, "We are in the protective embrace of the Almighty. We must remember that God's invisible hands are everywhere. May the faith in his protection grow stronger. Then we won't be anxious, we needn't fear anything or feel insecure.

God alone is our protector." Amma continues to impress this truth in us.

The ego is what prevents us from receiving God's grace. When we have wealth and friends, we might forget God. It is impossible to experience divine grace while individuality prevails. The ego disappears only when we find ourselves helpless. In those moments, we can enjoy such exalted experiences as we could never imagine. When we become worthy of receiving the Guru's grace, it will flow to us uninterruptedly.

3

Embodiment of Self-sacrifice

Scientists say that the whole universe is an effect of the flow of energy. The ancient *rishis* (sages) of Bharat proclaimed that the cosmos is the dance of Siva. Both were stating the same truth. However, the sages articulated the truth poetically. It is the dance of divine energy that manifests this beautiful universe of names and forms. Nevertheless, this universe is only a divine delusion. *Maya!* It is like the high-speed movements of a single dot of light that create colourful pictures on the television screen. But those images are not real, only the screen is. However, using the television screen, we can see many visuals and movies. Similarly, though the world is maya, it can be used to know the Supreme. If we know how to do so, this wonderful creation can help us remember God constantly. If we know how to move in tune with the flow of this divine energy, life will become effortless.

Amma often exhorts us, "Live in accordance with the laws of nature." To enjoy life, we must practise certain disciplines. Those practices are called dharma. This world has a mysterious power; it changes according to our imagination. A distorted mind will see only distortions everywhere, whereas mahatmas like Amma, who have perfect minds, behold only fullness and perfection everywhere. To see good everywhere, we must first purify the mind through rituals. All spiritual practices are meant to elevate us to *dhyana*, meditation. Even the natural scenery around us can uplift us to the state of meditation. We only need to connect it with God using imagination. Thus, we can awaken divine power anywhere and in anything.

In the early days, whenever I saw Amma sitting absorbed in meditation, I would be reminded of Sri Buddha. Watching Her sit still like a statue, without even the slightest breathing movements, devotees would be amazed. A previous chapter also referred to an incident in Amma's life that proves Her ability to cast away Her body as effortlessly as one would one's apparel. On one occasion, Her body became still like a lifeless body, without even a pulse, for a couple of hours. Afterwards, She sat up with a gentle smile.

Amma is a phenomenon that can never be fully understood. She is an ocean, the vastness and depth of which can never be measured with the intellect. She is an endless flow of love. She can be known through innocence. But to do so, one needs to have earned sufficient punya. Minds that are agitated by mere bookish knowledge can never perceive goodness anywhere. Such people project their own imperfections on others and turn this divine and beautiful earth into a battlefield.

I cannot describe how beautiful those early days were. Unable to bear staying away from Amma's divine presence, we used to spend days and nights in the courtyard of the kalari. Those were the days when we learned our first lessons in spirituality in Amma's holy presence. Whatever She did, we were inspired to emulate. To attain mental control, one needs to perfect the ability to sit in the same physical posture for a long time. When Amma sat in meditation, we, too, would sit around Her and meditate. When She sang bhajans, we, too, would join in the ecstasy of singing bhajans, forgetting everything else. Even if it was manual work, Amma would take the lead and show the way. This is how Amma directly instructed us in each and every aspect of spirituality.

If only we realise how valuable Amma's presence is, we can never stay away from Her. All those who criticised Amma became remorse stricken when they met Her in person. Their heads bowed down in reverence and their eyes welled up with tears. They had never imagined that there could be anyone with so many divine qualities. Amma's motherly affection was so overwhelming that She could gather into Her arms even the person who came to kill Her!

No scripture can create a realised master, but a realised master can create all scriptures. The disciple gets the golden opportunity to grasp the essence of the *sastras* (spiritual sciences) from the Master. Lord Krishna had no difficulty in imparting the *Bhagavad Gita* to Arjuna in just a few minutes, and that, too, in the battlefield! Even the battlefield could not impede the flow of Krishna's knowledge!

The Self-realised Master and the fully dedicated disciple commune in deep silence. One can never have enough of watching Amma sit still in deep meditation, like a statue of the Buddha. Once She sits in meditation and closes Her eyes, She may continue to sit like that for hours. Those seated nearby will continue to sit gazing at Amma's form. Later, Her unmoving form dawns in their pious hearts without much effort. This is how we picked up lessons in meditation from Amma. Unknowingly, we emulate all that Amma does. Those sitting near Amma become absorbed in meditation, oblivious to time and place.

One morning, when Amma sat in meditation, we joined Her. We remained seated until Amma's mother, Damayanti-amma, came in the evening and called us, saying, "Children, come and have some food!" When we told her that we would eat after Amma had emerged from Her meditation, Damayanti-amma objected. "Amma may not open Her eyes now. She has sat like this for several days together. But She won't like if She comes to know that you haven't had any food."

We got up and silently followed Damayanti-amma. Just then, we heard Amma's voice, "Naughty ones! So, you're all going to have food, leaving me here, are you? Very well, carry on!" Not knowing what to do or say, we stood helpless. Amma got up. Walking towards us, She said, "Amma shall serve you food."

She went to the kitchen. Returning with rice and curries, She mixed them, made balls from them and lovingly put them into our mouths with Her own hands. Such is Her compassion that She did not hesitate to forgo the bliss of meditation for the sake of serving Her children food. It occurred to us that all we did was to create more work for Her.

What inspired us to stay with Amma was not the prospect of a future ashram or knowledge of spirituality, only the love and affection of Amma, Mother of the Universe. Getting the rare opportunity to bathe in the Ganges of Knowledge, gushing down from the summits of spirituality, was transforming us totally.

Once a passer-by saw Amma spread a mat on the banks of the backwaters and then sit a little away from the mat to meditate. "Why has *Ammachikkunju* ('little Amma,' a name that elders used to affectionately called Her) spread the mat and sat on the bare ground?" he asked.

Sweetly smiling, Amma replied, "Once I start meditating, I'll open my eyes only after a long time. I thought, what if my children come; if I spread out the mat for them before beginning to meditate, they won't have to sit on the bare ground!"

The questioner stood still, unable to say anything. When we came to know about this from the devotee himself, we were not surprised, for such is Amma's nature.

Amma's life reflects only sacrifice. She reminds us that where there is love, there will be sacrifice. As love for God grows in us, no sacrifice will seem unbearable for us. Amma has incarnated as the epitome of self-sacrifice to teach us the greatness of sacrifice. Usually, it is the disciples who serve the Master. However, around Amma, there is a reversal of roles: the Guru serves Her disciples. Even today, Amma is engaged in activities that serve millions of people.

Medical science will tell us how hugging thousands of people can make one susceptible to infections and affect the body adversely. An incessant flow of water, however gentle it might be, can erode even huge boulders. However, Amma performs a whole lot of miracles with Her human body! Those who throw themselves on Her shoulders, as they wail in misery, are unaware of how much pain they are inflicting on Amma. But those that have watched it know. Quite a few people have seen Amma compassionately gathering to Her bosom, day after day, the leper shunned by the very mother who bore him. How many times the kalari has witnessed the scene of Amma licking his infected wounds and healing him with Her saliva.

Amma hugs everybody—those on the verge of death, those with contagious diseases, those with stinking wounds. Always, compassion is the only expression that one can see on her face. She showers on all an affection that even mothers cannot bestow. Amma's life perfectly exemplifies the aphorism, *'manava seva Madhava seva'*—'Service to man is service to God.'

One day, when I was alone, such thoughts about Amma's sacrifice welled up in my mind, and I composed the following song:

O primeval power, bliss of Brahman incarnate,
You have descended to the earth in the form of the Mother.
You can come to cleanse us of our sins and
to guide us along the true path.

Forgetting thoughts of caste and religion,
we stand united as Your children.
The walls of space and time have crumbled
and the dawn of peace has arrived.

O loving Mother, You have come to this dream world
to rescue and redeem us, Your children.
You are the Mother of the Universe
and the embodiment of self-sacrifice.

O Great Goddess, O Amriteswari,
You remove all sorrows and bestow good fortune.
Your darshan purifies us of all sins.
May I always enjoy that vision!

4

The Smile that Evokes Tears

For some mysterious reason,
Krishna's eyes were full of tears.
Has the valiant and lotus-eyed
Krishna ever cried?

This is how Ramapurathu Warrier, a famous Malayalam poet, described the reunion of Lord Krishna and Kuchela, the Lord's old classmate, in Dwaraka long after they had left their gurukul.

Never once had that ever-smiling lotus-face waned. Never had those eyes of Him who makes *jeevatmas* (individual souls) dance in bliss been moist. The Lord crying? It was more than Kuchela could bear! Kuchela's eyes, too, overflowed with tears. Nestling in the Lord's tight embrace, he bathed His body in tears.

Having heard the story of the Lord's eager, patient wait, Kuchela found it impossible to fathom His love. Was the Lord reassuring him that he was indeed Kubera (the Lord of Wealth), and not Kuchela (literally, the poor one)? True, the Lord's love and affection had indeed made him the richest one in the world! What greater thing was there to gain? Even as he journeyed back home, the image of the Lord's tearful eyes lingered ineffaceably in his mind.

The tale of Kuchela, whose mind soared to the supreme heights of samadhi, is a classic illustration of sublime love and devotion and the Lord's tender fondness for pious souls.

Countless lives, caught in the world's captivity, are unable to break free from its meshes. Boats caught in the breakers of samsara's (causal world's) seas are unable to reach the shores. After a long wait, the disciple reaches the Guru's feet and sees the smile on the Guru's face. The Guru's smile, playing below tearful eyes, makes you cry.

Lured by toys, the child loses itself in play under the blazing sun, unmindful of its mother's calls. When it becomes hungry and weary, he discards his toys and returns to his mother, crying. Seeing that, a tear-soaked smile spreads on the face of the mother, who is upset that she was unable to feed her dear son earlier. It is the smile of contentment.

During *Onam* (Kerala's harvest festival), every face is adorned with the flowers of such smiles. There is a saying, 'Partake of the Onam feast even if you have to sell off your property'. 'Enough' is said only when one has eaten to one's heart's content.

The story of little Ganapati's hunger is well known. All who attempted to sate his hunger had to admit defeat. Once, Kubera also tried to do so. He wanted to give a sumptuous feast to little Ganapati. Little Ganapati ate up enough food that could fill some ten thousand stomachs! Frustrated at still not having appeased his hunger, Ganapati started gulping all he could lay hands on. Terrified, Kubera fled. He took refuge with Lord Siva himself. Smiling, the Supreme Guru poured a handful of puffed rice into Ganesha's mouth. Lo, Ganesha was pacified!

Just a handful from His holy hand,
and Ganapati became full! Victory to Ganapati!

Most people in the world are like little Ganapati, roaming about with insatiable hunger for material gains. This appetite for indulgence can never be sated. Having obtained all, contentment will still remain elusive.

In fact, what each one of us seeks throughout life is God, the epitome of bliss. The seeking finally brings us to the Guru, who intones into our ears the *mahamantra*, *'Tat twam asi'*—'You are that.' In other words, the God, the essence of bliss, that was sought is none other than the seeker himself! To the mature disciple ready for renunciation, that truth becomes an experience.

The supreme Guru patiently waits for us to confess "Enough of the world!" The disciple understands that circumambulating the Guru is equivalent to circumambulating the world. The Guru patiently waits until this realisation deepens in the disciple—that, with the entire world under the Guru's feet, why wander about in the world anymore?

Sri Ramakrishna sang,

> *Where are you, my children?*
> *I'm sitting and waiting...*
> *Where are you, my children?*
> *Come here soon!*

While meditating in the kalari temple, Her inner eye seeing what was going to happen in the future, this question arose within Amma, too: "Where are my children?" She imagined that She was asking Devi this question. Then She saw clearly around Her an array of yogis engrossed in meditation. Thus, Amma beheld scenes from the unprecedented rendezvous about to occur in the future.

Long ago, during Onam, some of Amma's earliest disciples, too, witnessed that tear-soaked smile. Those scenes were also part of the drama of Her incarnation. Such a blessing comes once in aeons. God was waiting, the Guru was waiting, tears in Her eyes. The Ocean of Compassion was expecting Her children.

Many years ago, on the eve of holy *Tiruvonam* (the most important of the ten days of Onam), Amma affectionately asked us, "Children, will you come tomorrow?" Just a handful of people were present then. They were the youth thirsting to be with Amma, unable to return, having met Her. Enveloped by Her mesmerising love, they had renounced their worldly lives. I was one among those few.

Hearing Her question, we replied in unison, "Sure, we will." We promised Her that we would come. The story of the Emperor Mahabali who gave his word to Lord Vishnu come in the guise of Vamana is well known. When Vamana asked Mahabali for land covered by three paces for Him to sit in and meditate, it seemed a trifle for the king. "Three paces of land?" It was too small a demand, thought Mahabali, and smiled. Only when Vamana grew sky high did Mahabali realise that it would not be easy to fulfil the Lord's request. Bowing his head down was the only solution.

We, too, promised Amma that we would come. On *Tiruvonam*, it is customary for all family members to sit together and eat. People in every home look forward to this day. And so, none of us managed to get away from our homes on the morning of *Tiruvonam*. Though I had lunch early and set out from home, owing to the hustle and bustle of the Onam festivities, I had a tough time catching a bus. Finally, I reached the Ochira temple. From there, I walked some seven kilometres before finally reaching Amma's presence.

I looked around the kalari, but Amma was nowhere to be found. I searched for Her on the banks of the backwaters. Noticing a twirl of smoke in a corner, I walked there. The smoke was from a makeshift stove under a coconut tree. Just beside it was Amma, lying down on the sand. Grains of sand were stuck to the beads of sweat on her face. Only once could I bear to look at Amma lying down like that, her hands holding a *mudra* (mystic hand gesture), for the sight was heartrending. A little away a pot lay overturned. Crows were avidly feeding on the morsels of colocasia yam fallen out of it and scattered on the mud. Not understanding anything, I sat beside Amma, speechless. Bowing at Her feet, I apologised mentally.

Amma gently sat up. Meanwhile, Her other children started trickling in, one by one. Each one inquired about what had happened. Amma just smiled in response. After a while, She

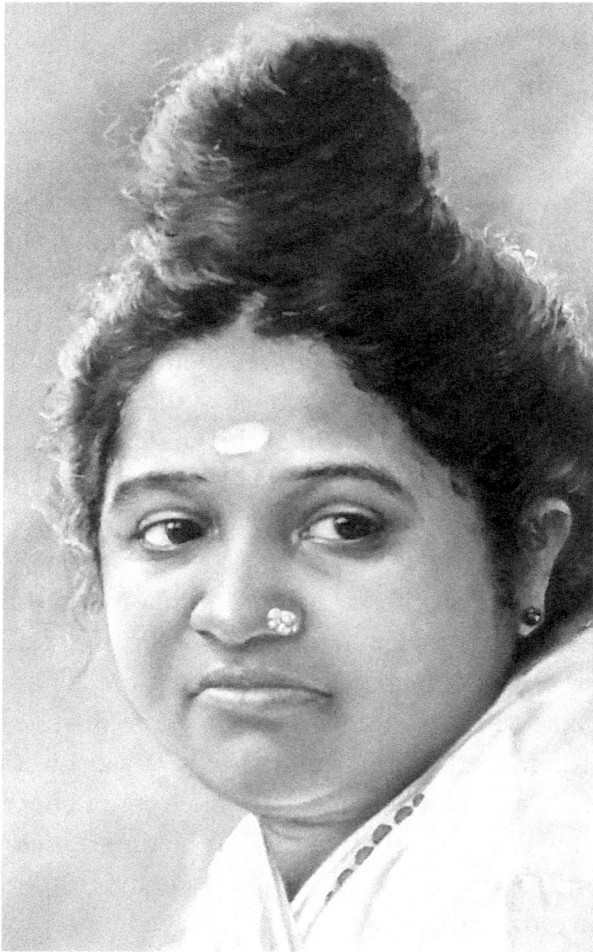

explained, "Children, you told me you would come in the morning, didn't you? After you left, Amma wondered, 'What will Amma give them when they came?' Amma secured some colocasia tubers from neighbouring homes and brought them in a basket. After preparing the stove, Amma peeled and washed the tubers, poured water into the pot and covered it with a lid, thinking that it would be cooked and ready by the time you children arrived. Amma then sat in meditation beside the stove.

"Amma waited for you for a long time. I even went to the jetty many times but saw no one. So Amma returned and sat beside the stove. The tubers were cooked and ready. If the pot were removed from the stove, the tubers would become cold, wouldn't it? So Amma kept the pot covered.

"'Why are my children late?' 'They may not have been allowed to leave their homes,' Amma found her own answers to the questions in her mind.

"Even after three o'clock, no one had come. Then Amma thought, 'It was not right to tell them to come today. Don't they have families? Would their mothers let them leave home on *Tiruvonam*? Isn't it the day when all the family members sit together to enjoy the Onam feast? In any case, I'm not their birth mother.'

"Amma lay down on the sand again. Presently, a crow came and perched on the pot, which tipped over, scattering the tubers on the ground. Only a few pieces were left in the pot. The crows tried to get those, too. Amma sprang up, thinking, 'What will I give my children now?' I became sad. I raised my hands to shoo the crows away, but then thought, 'Aren't they my children, too? Let them eat!' Amma lay down here itself. That is when you children started arriving, one by one."

All of us had brought with us packets of fried banana chips, an Onam delicacy. We spread them out before Amma. Amma opened them all and put the chips into our mouths. Amma watched us enjoying them. For some reason, tears had welled up in Her eyes. Seeing that we had noticed it, She tried to smile, a smile with tearful eyes! That smile made us all cry! Unable to bear the sight, I looked down. Even the setting sun hid its face in the sea! In that silence, we sat still, like rocks, for a long time.

I wondered, God, how can we impress upon the world the tale of Mother's love and Her children struggling to hold back their tears? As if in response, the lament of the waves that surged up on the Arabian Sea in the twilight continued to echo across the horizon.

5

Amma's Divine Flute

When I was a child, I longed to own the flute in the picture of little Krishna. That wish arose when I saw the flute in His hands. "If only I had a flute!" The intellect cannot grasp many of my experiences during that phase. There were days when I would call out to the picture, "Krishna, please give me that flute..." I did not understand why those who heard me burst out laughing! How beautiful those days were, when intellect was yet to develop, and when I still had the innocence of ignorance!

I was obsessed with thoughts of learning to play the flute somehow. These thoughts eventually led me to wanting to become Amma's flute. Earlier, I sought permission many times from my father to learn the flute. "Not now", was the reply. What if, carried away by music, I scored low marks in my school examinations—that was father's fear.

The day the festival of the Bhagavati Temple nearby commenced proved unforgettable for me. It was a *Kartika* day in the month of *Kumbham*. The temple premises were fully lit with *Kartika* lamps. Sitting in a corner was a man playing a flute. I went and stood beside him. He had many flutes arranged in front of him for sale. "How much are they?" I asked.

With great affection, he handed me a flute. "Pay me whatever you like," he said. I gave him all the coins I had with me then. With a smile, he wrapped the flute and gave it to me.

On reaching home, I tried to play the flute out of everyone's sight but produced no sound. It was then Grandmother came. Seeing me struggling to play the flute, Grandmother said, laughing, "Child, if you want to learn to play the flute, you need a teacher. You need a guru for mastering any knowledge."

"Will you obtain Father's permission for it, then?"

Hearing my question, Grandmother smiled and told me an easy way. "Don't worry, darling. Just go and pray at Evoor Krishna Temple. There's none more proficient in teaching one how to play the flute than Lord Krishna. You won't require any other teacher."

Grandmother knew the entire *Bhagavatam* by heart. Once she started recounting the Lord's stories, it would have been difficult for her to stop. She is not given to speaking hollow words. So I had no difficulty believing her words.

The very next day, I set out with a relative who lived next door. We walked almost three miles from home to reach Evoor Temple. However, the sanctum sanctorum had already been closed after the morning pujas. Standing with eyes closed in the temple courtyard for a long time, I spoke to Krishna about my requirement. I continued to pray while circumambulating the temple, too. Grandmother had given me money for the *pal payasam* (milk pudding) offering at the temple. As we had been late, we could not make that offering. Grandmother had also instructed me to return by foot.

I had not eaten that morning. While wearing my sandals, which I had left outside the temple wall, a large mango suddenly fell at my feet. I did not pick it up. Noticing this, a priest from the temple said, "Please take it, child. It fell from the mango tree in the temple compound. You mustn't have had any food, right? Take it as a gift from the Lord."

I bent down to pick up the mango. I then looked up to ask the priest about the pal payasam offering, but he was not to be seen there. Where had he disappeared? I asked my companion. He told me categorically that no priest had approached us. "Then what about the man I saw?"

After pondering over it, he said, "Must have been Krishna Himself. Such incidents are common here, child. It is proof that the Lord has heard your prayer."

Back home, I sat before Lord Krishna's picture and tried to play the flute. Musical notes started emanating from it effortlessly. After a few days' effort, I was able to play short bhajans. Later, playing the flute became part of my daily routine. Today, I know that the Lord had been training me in a ritualistic art without anybody's knowledge. I see it as the beginning of my meditation practice. I have not tried to play the flute before anyone for recognition, though I have played before friends while in college. I started playing on public platforms only after meeting Amma. Today I am engaged in striving to become Amma's flute. I have only one prayer to Amma. "Please make me Your flute!"

Amma, Please Make Me Your Instrument!

I am reminded of Vivek, a Japanese devotee of Amma, who once submitted a prayer. Prior to becoming an ashram inmate, Vivek used to work as an English teacher in Japan. Whenever he managed to obtain leave from work, he would go to see Amma. He also used to accompany Her on Her tours abroad. An incident that happened during Amma's American tour was a clear illustration of the spirit of total dedication.

A few years ago, Amma's final programme in North America was in progress in Boston. Vivek approached me for help. He was returning to Japan from Boston. He wanted to say "Amma, please make me Your instrument" in Malayalam, and asked me to teach him how to say it. I taught him the words. Saying that he had learnt it, Vivek joined the darshan line. A little later, Vivek came running to me once again: "Swamiji, I forgot the words. Will you teach me once again?" I taught him yet again. He also wrote the words down on his palm, lest he forget. He then joined the line again.

Curious to see what would happen when he was with Amma, I went and stood behind Her. Vivek prostrated before Amma and then became speechless! I realised that he had forgotten everything. He tried to read the writing on his palm but couldn't as his spectacles had been removed. Unable to say anything, Vivek looked like a statue, with bowed head. His eyes filled with tears. I also stood silent, looking on. Amma turned back and smiled at me, his teacher. Onlookers also smiled though they did not know the story. In a loud voice, Amma told Vivek, "Now, you have become a real instrument!" Should those words be interpreted, one could write a whole book!

The words of mahatmas are aphorisms. An instrument cannot speak. It surrenders itself completely to the musician. From that surrender, divine music is born. When we develop such an attitude of surrender, miraculous transformations will happen in our lives, too. Life will become as sweet as an immortal melody.

The incident mentioned earlier was the beginning of a total transformation in Vivek's life. Thereafter, he became a beloved teacher to students of Amrita Vishwa Vidyapeetham (Amrita University). Having dedicated his life to service, he continues striving to become an instrument in Amma's hand. Even now Vivek has only one prayer: "Amma, please make me Your instrument."

6

Born To Lead

Amma's life is a saga of self-sacrifice. Whereas we prioritise our own happiness, Amma is never concerned about Her own pleasures and comforts. Her only wish is to ensure peace and happiness for all.

The following incident took place years ago. I was staying with Amma in the ashram. A group of devotees from Ernakulam came to meet Amma and requested Her to send a *brahmachari* (male celibate aspirant) to the Ernakulam ashram. The construction of the new ashram had just been completed. The devotees suggested my name.

Amma sent for me immediately. She said, "Sreemon (that is how Amma used to call me affectionately), these people have come to take you to Kochi (Ernakulam). You must leave today itself, alright?"

I only smiled but did not say anything in reply. I did not know what had transpired between Amma and the Ernakulam ashram committee members and did not take the matter seriously.

In those days, I used to play the harmonium for Amma during bhajans; there was no one else in the ashram to play the harmonium. So I figured that She would not send me anywhere. That evening, I played the harmonium as usual during Amma's bhajans. Amma did not say anything about going to Ernakulam thereafter. Three months later, the committee members came again and reminded Amma about their request. Amma asked, "Didn't Sreemon go?"

"Not yet," they said in unison. Amma sent for me. When I arrived, She admonished me in front of them.

I could not imagine staying away from Amma, but there was no alternative. It was Amma's order. How could She be so cruel? I decided to leave for Kochi that very day. Not waiting to say a word to Amma, I took my sling bag and left for Ernakulam.

I had never even dreamt that I would have to re-enter the world after having renounced everything in it and come to Amma. I had imagined then that Amma would make us perform *tapas* (intense spiritual austerities) in some Himalayan forest and thus transport us to the abode of God. After coming to Amma, I had prayed that never again should I be made to see the tainted world of selfishness. I had even forgotten that such a world existed. After meeting Amma, the hands of the clock did not appear to have moved, and time seemed to have stopped. The past few years had seemed like moments only. Time is said to move fast in heaven. How true, I thought. Engrossed in such thoughts, I did not realize that the vehicle had reached Kochi. The Queen of the Arabian Sea, which had seemed like a dreamland during my college days, now seemed to have become less attractive.

No one had known of my arrival. None of the committee members were there. I sat, lost in thought, in the solitude of the ashram. I could not sleep that night. How could Amma send me here? Did She not know how much my mind ached? Every thought that emerged within disturbed me. Sitting on the ashram terrace, I gazed helplessly into the night sky. In the distance, thick black smoke was rising up from the chimney of some factory and spreading across the horizon. At least, the factory has chimneys, I thought! I did not know how to stop my heart from being consumed by the thoughts smouldering in the mind. I sat there until daybreak, not able to share my pangs of grief with anyone. As I penned down the silent plaintive notes of my mind, I could hardly see what I wrote for the tears.

O Lalita, O Eternal Mother,
do not make me an orphan.
This world, teeming with orphans and the destitute,
is an abode of endless sorrow.

Many are the fragrant flowers
in the garden of Your mind.
O Goddess of my heart, aren't You aware
Of the grief that this wilting flower feels?

How many dream-like years have passed
in search of Your sacred feet!
O Mother of compassion, You have still not shown me mercy.
When will You bless me with Your gaze of compassion?

After I finished writing these lines, I sat there with eyes closed. Someone came and roused me with a gentle touch. Startled, I turned round. It was Sajan, from the neighbouring house. He said that Amma was on the phone. Why would She call? I eagerly went to answer the call. Amma asked, "Son, why did you go to Kochi? Amma wasn't serious! Come back soon. Amma didn't scold you to hurt you but to make those committee children happy. You didn't understand that, did you? Darling son, did you feel very sad?"

Hearing Her words of consolation, all my sorrows melted away. I returned to Amritapuri that very morning.

Months rolled by. The severity of the monsoon eased a little. One day, I was roused from my meditation by the caress of the sun's golden rays. I had sat down for meditation at 2 a.m. and had not been aware of the passing of time. This was, no doubt, Amma's blessings at work. The first experience of inner bliss had led me to a long silence. I spent most of my time in spiritual practices and became witness to a series of miraculous experiences.

Even the grains of sand in the ashram courtyard are vibrant with pulsations of holy names and mantras day and night. How could Amma's children ever leave this place?

While sitting alone under a coconut tree in the courtyard after the morning meditation, the Ernakulam ashram committee members came again. This time, they came straight towards me and apologised for the trouble they had caused me. They had not realised that living away from Amma would be so painful for me. They said, "Please forgive us. We thought only about our own happiness. We should have considered your feelings also. It was our mistake. Only now have we understood the depth of your love for Amma. No, we don't want to be happy at the cost of your happiness!"

Many of them had tears in their eyes. I was moved. Their words continued to ring in my heart again and again. "We thought only about our own happiness. We should have considered your feelings also…"

It occurred to me that I, too, should have done so. I should not have acted as I did. I had made them unhappy for the sake of my own happiness. That was not right at all. I am not supposed to expect happiness. The experience of Godhood is only for those who renounce happiness and pleasures.

One cannot enjoy swimming in the sea right away. One must first be trained. So also, the nature of creation is such that one cannot obtain happiness from it easily. It is impossible for sensualists. Spiritual training is required. Sacrifice is needed. This is what Amma is showing us. She is instilling in us lessons in sacrifice. She spends Her days and nights bringing happiness to the world. Even Her prayers are for the wellbeing of people all over the world. I ought to follow Amma's path.

I recollected the story of Amma's life. In Her teens, She learnt tailoring. Her aim was to make some money from it to help the poor. The tailoring class was near a church. She would spend Her free time in the church or the adjoining cemetery. One day, as She stood gazing at the image of the Crucifixion, the Vicar asked Her, "Child, I have been observing you for several days. You are always praying. I tried to gather more information about you and asked many people. I heard that you are a child endowed with extraordinary abilities. I came to know that everyone gives you only pain but still you love them all. I see in your eyes the flood of compassion Lord Jesus had for humanity. How do you bear this burden?"

In response, Amma asked the Vicar, "How did Christ endure the agony of the crucifixion? Where there is love, even troubles become blissful. What is special about my suffering? So many people struggle and suffer untold misery in this world. I constantly hear the lamentations of the destitute. How can I be happy when so many people are living in the midst of misery and agony? I love to struggle and know how to enjoy it. I consider it God's grace."

Hearing Amma's reply, the Vicar became emotional. With folded hands, he said, "This child will become great in future. I have no doubt about it!"

I recalled Amma's words. "How can I be happy when so many people are living in the midst of misery and agony?" Everyone thinks of one's own happiness alone. If we are ready to accept sorrow, more divine grace will flow towards us, and we will reach God faster.

I slowly walked towards Amma's room. I fell at Her feet and said, "Amma, I am willing to go to Ernakulam."

Hearing my words, Amma looked at me and said, "Why? Amma didn't tell you to go."

That was right. Amma had not told me to. "Henceforth, I shall not accord much importance to my happiness, Amma. I am ready to sacrifice my happiness for the sake of others' happiness. Amma, isn't that what You are teaching us through Your life?"

Smiling, Amma said, "Son, I have been waiting to hear this from you. Even when you are physically away from me, you will not go without love and affection. You will never be away from me. Wherever you go, there will be people to love you. You will get Amma's love everywhere!"

Her words came true. I was convinced of it from the experiences that I had later. Wherever in the world I went, I received Amma's love.

When I returned to Kochi, I was far from sad. Amma's words of wisdom became an inspiration. In the days that followed, I continued to experience the fulfilment and bliss of self-sacrifice. Sitting before Amma's photograph in the Kaloor ashram in Kochi, I penned down a few lines in my diary.

I sought the embodiment of bliss.
I sought the embodiment of immortality.
I realised that the dispeller of ignorance,
that stream of knowledge
was none other than my own Self.

Those with eyes open saw not Your form.
Those with keen ears heard not Your voice.
Close the eyes and ears.
She, who resides in the heart, will dawn within.

You are the real fortune that is attained
when all fortunes are discarded.
You are the beauty one beholds
when all other attractions are forsaken.

Bestow on me the strength to open the inner eye.
Make me intoxicated with divine bliss.
Until the day You dawn within,
I shall immerse myself in tears.

7

The Arrival of a Siddhayogi

A *siddha yogi* (accomplished yoga master) started coming to the ashram regularly. He was a well-built man with long hair and a beard. Right from the start, he was disliked, and many in the ashram viewed him with suspicion. He would not go for Amma's darshan but sit instead in some corner to meditate. Noticing him meditating, a few people flocked around him. When he opened his eyes once in a while, he would talk to those assembled there. He would give them advice on certain matters. This created some confusion among devotees. Some became very angry. They felt that he was trying to mislead devotees. "We must drive this man away from here," they said.

By and by, he started going for Amma's darshan. Whenever he came, Amma would give him a lot of time. Seeing this, people started becoming more jealous and wanted to prevent him somehow from coming to the ashram. One day, he invited Amma to his ashram. Many stories started circulating about him. Some said that he was a black magician, who was trying to entice Amma to his ashram, and that if he succeeded, his ashram could attract fame. There were many such speculations. People began to detest the very sight of him. Only Amma smiled whenever She saw him. The angrier people became towards him, the more loving Amma became towards him.

After he invited Amma to his ashram, devotees went to Amma and said, "Amma, please don't go there. Even his coming here has been disturbing our minds."

Amma began asking everyone's opinion. "Amma has been invited to his ashram. What will I do? What should I say?"

All the devotees said, "Amma, please do not go there under any circumstance!" For two or three days, everyone was telling Amma the same thing. And thus, those who had been hailing

Amma as Jagadeeswari, the Goddess of the Universe, began advising Her.

Finally the day arrived when Amma had said She would make known Her decision. On that day, the siddha yogi arrived earlier than usual with a few people from his ashram. With bated breath, everyone observed him talk to Amma for a lot of time during darshan. After prostrating to Her, he said, "Amma, please don't say You won't come. I have already told everyone that Amma will visit our ashram."

Amma said, "I'll come, son."

The devotees present stood as if thunderstruck. Later they asked, "Amma, why did You agree to go there?"

Amma said, "What can I do? When invited, can I say I won't come? Children, I cannot hurt anyone."

Someone interrupted and shot Amma a question, "Why do You give so much importance to such people?"

Hearing the question, all looked at Amma, for he had asked the very question that was on everyone's mind. Amma gravely replied, "I am everyone's Mother. Don't forget that."

The day of Her visit to the ashram arrived. Some devotees went to Her and whispered to her, "Ammachikkunju, when you reach there, don't eat any food they give you. If they offer you milk, don't drink it!" Thus they tutored Her before She left. Everyone was anxious about losing Amma. What if black magic was performed on Her? The devotees followed Her like bodyguards.

As soon as She reached the ashram, Amma violated all the pacts. She went into the siddha yogi's puja room where food, milk all other items had been arranged as offerings. "All potent with black magic," muttered one bodyguard. Amma ate all the food kept and even drank the milk. As we stood watching, She poured the remaining food and milk into the mouths of those present. What to do? As the offerings were from Amma, they were *prasad* (consecrated). How can one reject prasad? The devotees were in a dilemma. They stood with the expression of a child struggling to gulp some bitter potion. Amma said, "Don't worry , children. This is prasad."

Amma then toured the ashram premises. She liked it very much. Finally, She said, "We are not leaving today. This place is full of sacred groves. It is an ideal place to meditate." Amma entered into a grove and sat down to meditate. Even hours later, She had not opened Her eyes. Some of the devotees said, "Looks like we've lost our Ammachikkunju. The black magic seems to have worked. We won't get Her back for sure."

When Amma opened Her eyes, everyone stood around Her. She started giving darshan to the local people who had arrived after learning about Amma's visit. As usual, all sat near Her and sang bhajans.

Amma left after two days. The scene of the siddha yogi bidding Amma farewell stunned everyone. After offering Her *dakshina* (ceremonial token of reverence) and prostrating to Her, he stood with palms joined prayerfully. His eyes were brimming with tears. We were deeply moved as we watched Amma compassionately wipe away his tears.

After returning to Amritapuri, Amma said, "Don't jump to conclusions. Not everything you hear is true. Don't approach anything with prejudice. Children, try to see the good in others. Those who seek evil can never find good in anyone. They will also never find peace."

We should keep our hearts so pure that they become a shrine for God. Through love and sacrifice, our lives should be dedicated as offerings for the good of the world. Amma continues to give this message through Her words and deeds, with the resolve that we merge with Almighty God at the soonest.

8

Syllables that Vanquish Death

All human beings dream of good luck and long for good fortune. But they are unaware of the fortunes they have already been blessed with. According to our *acharyas* (teachers), we are already immensely blessed as it is difficult to obtain three things: a human birth (*manushyatwam*), the desire for spiritual liberation (*mumukshatwam*), and the company of a self-realised Master (*mahapurushasamsrayam*). We have been blessed with these three things, which are difficult to obtain. But as our minds are preoccupied with so many desires, we are not aware of the magnitude of these blessings. Deep in our heart, we all yearn for liberation. Yet we hanker after material objects and sense pleasures. Even if God were to appear before us, ready to grant us liberation, we may well tell Him to defer the blessing! We would rather seek boons that fulfil our immediate desires.

But the truth is that, as soon as one desire is satisfied, another one quickly takes its place, like the never ending waves of the ocean. These desires destroy our peace of mind. Only when the waves of desire subside can we truly be free. As for liberation, we might imagine that we need to give up our body to be liberated. But mahatmas show us that it is not so. Liberation is a state of existence in which the sorrows of this world have no power to affect us.

Amma says that the mind is like a key. Turn it to one side, and it locks us in and becomes a cause of bondage. Turn it to the other side, and it sets us free. The mind is capable of creating as well as solving problems.

Often, we do not realise how fortunate we are. Almost always, people talk only about their problems. They forget the grace and the many gifts they have received. They brood over what they do not have and end up sorrowful. Once in a while, I visit patients at the AIMS (Amrita Institute of Medical Sciences) Hospital. One day, I asked a twelve-year-old girl, "What is your life's greatest dream?"

She smiled and said to me with twinkling eyes, "I am eagerly waiting for the day I can walk to the restroom alone without anybody's help. That is my biggest dream." She was not even dreaming about getting discharged from the hospital.

Another young man told me, "I wish I could breathe without oxygen cylinders. That is my greatest desire."

Yet another person, who is sightless, lives with the hope of being able to behold this beautiful world one day. We have all these blessings which some people only dream of!

If we have a healthy body, we can perform good actions and earn *punya* (spiritual merit). To do so, we need to live a dharmic life. We need to hold steadfastly to Truth. Truth is that which is eternal. God is eternal truth and beauty. But man, preoccupied with the fleeting pleasures of the world, is caught in the endless cycle of birth and death. We need to break free of this cycle. We need to gain victory over death and be one with the Great Guru. So the rishis prayed to Lord Siva, who is Mrityunjaya, the conqueror of death. The mantra they chanted is called the *Maha Mrityunjaya Mantra*:

> *Om tryambakam yajaamahe*
> *Sugandhim pushti vardhanam*
> *Urvaarukamiva bandhanaat*
> *Mrityor muksheeyamaamritaat*

I meditate on that Divine Being, who embodies the powers of will, knowledge and action. I surrender myself completely before Him. I pray to Him, who manifests as fragrance in the flower and who constantly nourishes the plant of life. Like an adept gardener, may He free me of all forces detrimental to my physical, mental and spiritual well-being. May the Eternal Being that dwells within me deliver me from disease, death and decay and make me one with Him.

Knowledge gained through the five senses is limited. To know things, it is not enough to be able to see with our physical eyes. To know all there is to know, the eye of wisdom needs to open. The Guru is one in whom the eye of wisdom is open. He is Siva, the Lord of Destruction. What does Siva destroy? Our ego, worldliness and negative thinking. He burns them to ashes. The Guru aims to remove the sorrow, ignorance, ego and darkness within us. Siva, the Lord of Destruction, destroys our *vasanas*, the subtle mental tendencies.

Siva is a Yogi. Kamadeva, the god of desire, shot his arrows at Siva. But Siva burnt Kama to ashes. Afterwards, He entered wedlock. The wedding of a person who has burnt all his desires in the fire of wisdom is not like that of an ordinary person. Although the masculine and feminine principles exist within every individual, ordinary people need the presence of other men and women to awaken the latent aspects in them. But yogis know that they are *ardhanareeshwara*, a perfect balance of the masculine and feminine. Masculinity implies valour, and femininity implies love and compassion. An individual becomes whole only when both these unite in him in perfect balance. If we observe Amma, we will find in Her valour like we can find in no man. We also find in Her motherhood like we can find in no woman. Only one who has awakened the innate masculinity and femininity in equal measure can perceive wholeness or perfection. In other words, Siva was entering into wedlock with His own inner *Sakti*, Female Principle, and not another woman apart from Himself.

Siva is *Kalakala* (*Kala* of *Kala*), i.e. Kala (God of Death) of Kala (Time). He is the destroyer of time. Siva is One who has conquered death and time. Time eats up our lives. We are all at the mercy of Time. But jnanis are capable of controlling death. Jnanis like Amma are born of their own will and cast away their physical frames at their own will, whereas people like us are born helpless and die helpless, with no control over anything. The strength to overcome death is not something acquired from the outside. We have been sent to this earth with that potential within ourselves.

The *Maha Mrityunjaya* mantra awakens that potential within. It is capable of eliminating all fear. This mantra was born spontaneously from an outpouring of compassion in the rishi's mind as he witnessed the untold suffering of human beings relying on the fleeting objects of the world for happiness. This mantra is not just meant for extending one's earthly lifespan! The solution to all our misfortunes and illnesses is surrendering to the three-eyed Siva. Humans have only two eyes. The mysteries of life in this world cannot be pierced with such limited vision. Moreover, physical eyes often show us untruths and weaknesses. Relying on others with such limited vision, therefore, cannot take us very far.

Therefore the rishi says, '*Tryambakam yajamahe.*' I worship the three-eyed Siva. I take refuge in the great truth, which is deathless and timeless. Why do I do this? '*Sugandhim pushti vardhanam.*' The *rishi* prays for fragrance—not the ordinary fragrance but the fragrance of purity of heart, spiritual strength and inner beauty. When our third eye, i.e. the eye of wisdom, opens, waves of peace will start flowing incessantly from our being towards all of creation. It is this fragrance the rishi prays for. He also prays for all kinds of success, abundance, vitality and perpetuation. '*Urvarukamiva bandhanaat.*' The cucumber gourd is attached to its plant by a small stem. Unlike other fruits, it doesn't fall off even when fully ripe. It requires a deft gardener to separate it from its plant, softly but surely. The wheel of *samsara* (cycle of birth and death) is the stem that connects our body, which encapsulates the jivatma to the unseen *paramatma chaitanya* (supreme effulgence). Samsara has its hold on us right from the moment we are born. '*Mrityor muksheeyamaamritaat.*' The rishi prays, "Just as the ripe fruit is finally free of the plant, may I be freed from the grip of death." This is not only a prayer for freedom from the grip of death but also one asking to be never kept away from the bliss of immortality. The rishi spontaneously offers this prayer and takes refuge in the Great Guru, who is beyond the three *gunas* (attributes) and who is the embodiment of *Om*, the primordial mantra.

Siva is present before us in the form of Amma. It is God Himself who incarnates as the Guru to guide sincere seekers. God's grace assumes the form of a Guru. To see the Guru is to see God Himself for the Guru is ever one with God. The Guru's presence invokes devotion in our hearts and purifies us. Amma is an ocean of compassion, wisdom and bliss. She is the helmsman of our souls, an eternal wellspring of joy. She can eliminate all our sorrows and obstacles and raise us to Godhood. Before She can do so, we need to take refuge in Her in a spirit of total dedication. May Amma bless us with complete surrender.

9

Essence of Perfection

Man can attain the state of perfection, also called God-realisation, while still in the body. This is the message the rishis of Bharat gave the world thousands of years ago. Amma constantly reminds us, "Man is not one meant to die and blend with the soil like beasts. His destiny is to become enraptured by the blissful experience of God-realisation."

What is this Self-realisation? It is liberation from all bondage, all sorrows, and all limitations. To understand the sweetness, beauty and greatness of God-realisation, it is enough to observe Amma for some time. The perfection, attractiveness and spontaneity of Her actions are not to be found anywhere else. At darshan time, unparalleled motherly compassion, which no other mother in the world can offer, flows from Amma. During Devi Bhava, we can see the endless lilas of Jagadeeswari. As a Guru, She assumes the form of a relentless and uncompromising Sadguru. In the midst of children, She becomes even more childlike than the children themselves. One can only watch in wonder the infinite facets of Amma's divinity. She also gives us the strength to behold the whole cosmos in Her. Her array of devotees demonstrates the truth that what the yogis longed to earn through ages, the *gopis* (milkmaids) of Vrindavan earned very soon.

Many devotees coming to Amma can be heard saying, "We came to ask Amma many things but forgot everything during darshan! It is only later that we realized that we hadn't asked anything!" In Amma's, presence we forget everything. We simply experience the bliss of the Self. And then all sorrows disappear. Once, a woman who came for Amma's darshan handed over her three-month-old baby to Amma, who laid the infant on Her shoulder and hugged its mother. Seeing the mother walk away after darshan, forgetting to take her daughter from Her hands,

Amma started laughing! Amma called out loudly, "It seems that daughter is in samadhi! Seeing Amma, she forgot everything, even her baby!"

Once I asked Amma, "Amma, thousands of devotees come to see You every day. How are You able to see their minds?" Amma said, "Son, as far as I am concerned, there are no 'others'. All are Amma. Where then is the difficulty in understanding their minds?"

I recalled lines from Amma's poem *Ananda Veethi* (The Path of Bliss):

From that day onwards, I could see nothing as separate.
Everything was my own Self.

Having attained the non-dualistic experience that all is One, it is not possible to see anything as separate from oneself. Mahatmas have experienced the truth that the same divine effulgence permeates everything. Those who have had the chance to witness the elaborate lilas of the incarnation are blessed indeed.

A big problem with youth today is boredom. They complain that they get bored all the time. They resort to intoxicants to find peace. Sometimes, they indulge in criminal acts. Once, a little girl was heard telling her grandmother, "How could Grandma live so many years in this world? I'm already bored!"

All objects in this world induce boredom. Even that which seems most attractive today will become boring tomorrow, for sure. There is only one that will never bore: God. The rishis described God as *puratana* (ancient), which also means 'ever new'.

No one complains of boredom around Amma. No matter how long one watches Her, it is never enough. The longing for Her presence never ends. Irrespective of age, all become like small children longing to be with Mother.

Once, after a reception accorded to Amma in northern Kerala, thousands of people thronged for Her darshan. The organisers repeatedly announced through loudspeakers that those who have had darshan once should not come again. People were specially appointed to ensure that no one came for darshan more than once. In addition, police were monitoring the situation. Amid that hustle and bustle, Amma tapped on a man's head and said, "Naughty one! How many times have you come?" Then turning to people around Her, She laughed and said loudly, "It's the third time this son is coming for darshan! His mind has become fully absorbed in Amma." Amma could recognise him in the midst of thousands upon thousands. She recognizes not only our physical form but also knows our mental constitution. People coming from the boring world and seeking the torrent of love are in no mind to return!

One day, as I was standing near the doorstep of Amma's room, an ashram resident came to me and asked, "Swami, why you standing here?"

I said, "To see Amma."

Then he said, "But weren't you with Her during Her overseas tour?"

It was then that it occurred to me that the brahmachari had not seen Amma for many months. Having been with Her all the while, nevertheless, I still felt the same excitement as I did when I met Her for the first time. No wonder the rishis said, "ever new". Off and on, I remember that those who came earlier ought to make way for the devotees arriving later. Perhaps that is why Amma gave us many responsibilities; so that we would not find the time to feel sad! The truth is that if memories of

Amma hurt us when we are physically away from Her, then the sweetness of that agony will help to deliver us from material conditioning. Dispassion will come easily to one who has such love for the Guru. No object in the world will be able to attract such a person. The Guru, who is the embodiment of infinite compassion, will certainly shower divine grace on one who takes refuge at Her lotus feet.

We are ready to undergo any sacrifice for the sake of enjoying Amma's proximity. This is proof that the divine qualities within are awakening. Rain or shine, thousands of people are ready to wait long hours for Amma's darshan. We need no other proof to know that this incarnation who attracts everyone to Her, irrespective of age, is verily Jagadeeswari.

An incident that occurred during one of Amma's foreign tours comes to the mind. She arrived in a place called Schweibenalp in Switzerland at dusk. There were no programmes on the day of Her arrival. Thousands of people had arrived much in advance to stay there for more than four days and participate in the programmes. Those who couldn't get rooms had already set up small tents outside. The devotees received Amma, singing the bhajan *'Amma Amma Taye'*. Amma made all of them happy by walking amidst them, and touching their heads and hands, thus giving them a lightning darshan. After loudly saying "Namah Sivaya" with folded hands and looking at everybody gathered, Amma walked towards the building in which She would stay.

A double-storeyed building had been specially arranged for Her stay. As soon as She entered Her room, Amma said that someone was inside. Swamini checked the place thoroughly but saw nobody. An hour must have elapsed. Amma parted the curtains covering the wall and window of the room. There, in the space between the cupboard and window was a small girl clad in a white dress! She must have been less than ten years old. When Amma went up to her, the girl burst into tears. Amma laid her on Her lap and consoled her for a long time. When she stopped crying, Amma asked, "Daughter, why did you come here?"

The girl said, "To see Amma." She couldn't wait until darshan the next day! So she had hid herself in this room before Amma came, standing without moving or making any noise for hours on end! Like the boons that Nachiketa (a character from the *Puranas*), who stood waiting for three days to see Lord Yama (the god of death), obtained, the innocent mind of the girl must have become uplifted by Amma's shower of love.

Mahatmas perceive the Divine Self in all creation. They know that the entire universe is within. They experience the truth that nothing is separate from oneself. Therefore, they are able to see everyone as their own and love them so.

When the astronauts who first set foot on the moon returned to the earth, journalists asked them, "What was your first thought on looking at the earth from the moon?"

Their replies were identical. "Seeing the earth risen in the full splendour of blue radiance, seemingly several times larger than the moon as seen from the earth, the first thought was, 'How beautiful my earth!" My home, my wife, my children, my country... such thoughts did not come to mind."

The thought that the whole earth was mine occurred at exalted heights. Similarly, having scaled the exalted heights of divine experience, the thought that the whole universe is mine also dawns. Let us take refuge in Amma. What cannot be gained from anywhere in the world can be gained from the Guru.

Whatever is gained from the world is impermanent. Whether we deserve it or not, the Guru can grant us material wealth. However, the Guru cannot bestow spiritual experience on us unless we are deserving of it. Rather, it is not something to be given but to be taken from the Guru. The Guru's shower of grace is always available. Let us prepare ourselves to receive it.

10

Ecstasy of Eternal Freedom

Life is a chain of problems. As soon as one problem is solved, the next one arrives! Thus, we go on solving problems. We are so busy solving problems all the time that we miss the chance to enjoy life.

Amma says, "If we can cry for God, we won't have to cry lifelong." Even if we live in the midst of material prosperity, one day it will leave us. It will fade away even from our memory, like a beautiful dream! Our material gains are only as important as a lottery prize won in a dream! Of what use is becoming a millionaire in a dream!

I visited a patient in the Critical Care Unit of the AIMS hospital. He had been a millionaire. He told me that he had lived a privileged life of pleasures. But what of it! It was only then that he seemed to have grasped the import of the words of Ezhuthachan (saint, father of modern Malayalam, and author of *Addhyatma Ramayanam*): "Pleasure and pain are equal once the duration of the experience has ended!" The patient lamented that even the memories of his luxurious past had disappeared! With trembling lips, the old man mumbled: "I can't eat anything now. My vision has dimmed considerably. I can't even breathe without life support. Lying like this, I'm as good as dead! Even my relatives don't care to visit me even once. I now realise what a waste my whole life has been. I gained nothing from my long life of extravagance and luxury. And here I am, awaiting death like an animal!"

These were the last words of a world-famous scientist: "All my life, I have studied the outer universe. However, I remained totally ignorant of my inner world. And now, with no control over even my own body, I having to die like a mere animal!" These words are a stern warning to the intellectuals who pursue material achievements alone.

In the final moments of life, our intellect and logic will not be of much help. Grace alone will be our sole refuge. We must succeed in earning grace through virtuous deeds. If we do so, even death will be a beautiful experience. Death is not the end of life. It is just the beginning of another life. To those who have lived a dharmic life, even death will be a divine experience.

According to the *Puranas* and the *Atharva Veda* (the fourth Veda), there are fourteen worlds: seven higher worlds and seven nether worlds. In addition, a number of hells exist, too. According to the *Bhagavata Purana*, heaven is where punya is exhausted, and hell, where sin is exhausted. Only on earth can we accumulate punya. Even *devas* (spiritually evolved divine beings) pray for a human body so that they may earn punya! To reach the godly world or attain God-realisation, we must have earned a lot of punya. Only then can we break free of the strong gravitational pull of the worlds of experiences. Sadly, even after having been born human, we do not appreciate the value of the human birth and the human body. The rishis strove to go beyond heaven and hell. They strove to know that One who is beyond all realms of experiences, who is witness to everything, who is the Self.

Our present knowledge of life is very limited. As a result, we do not understand the realities of life. In reality, creation is a divine delusion.

Once, a few journalists obtained special permission to visit heaven. A guard opened the portals of heaven. Inside, the journalists were greeted by the sight of its occupants snoring away! The shocked journalists asked the guard, "What nonsense is this? Why is everyone sleeping here?"

The guard replied, "All are happy here. There's no need to do any work here. That's why they are sleeping!"

The journalists remarked, "What a boring place! It's as lifeless as a graveyard. Could you please show us hell?"

"Sure!" said the guard. He led them to another place and opened the portals of hell to them. They were greeted by beautiful sights of people drinking liquor, laughing merrily, singing and dancing! The entire place was teeming with life.

The journalists loved the place. One of them asked, "Will you let me live here forever? I don't wish to return!"

"No," said the guard, "Only the dead may stay here."

Hearing this, the journalist told the doorkeeper, "If so, please arrange to bring me here instead of heaven when I die!"

The guard replied, "Oh, don't worry about that. If you continue doing what you're already doing—finding fault with others, and threatening others—you'll end up here for sure!"

The journalist returned to the earth. When he died, he was escorted to the gateway to hell. When the sentinel opened the doors, the journalist started screaming in terror! He came face to face with horrendous scenes straight out of a horror movie: tortures inflicted by demons, raging fires, thousands of venomous snakes, ferocious animals as well as heartrending wails and heartless guffaws. "What's this?" the journalist demanded in shock.

"Why, this is hell!" the doorkeeper replied.

"But you showed me a different hell the last time," protested the journalist!

"I'm sorry", the guard said, "That hell was meant only for tourists. This is the real one!"

We may have many dreams about life. However, it is only when we enter into the realities of life that we come to understand the real nature of the world, the sad truth that this world is full of misery and suffering. Reality is very different from expectation.

The pleasures of heaven, too, are transitory. Therefore the rishis did not attach much importance to the heavenly worlds. They resolved to rise above them. They said, "Transcend the earth and heaven! Know what our goal ought to be: Freedom! You must become totally free! To do so, embrace the state of perfection."

How can we do this? With God's help. The special hugs of a Sadguru like Amma absorb and purify our karma. But we must sustain that purity through spiritual practices and selfless actions.

There is a beautiful poem in Hindi. The poet sings,

> *Kaun kehte hain Bhagvan aate nahin?*
> *Tum Meera ke jaise bulaate nahin!*
>
> *Who says the Lord doesn't come?*
> *You don't call Him like Meera did!*

Whenever the great devotee Meera called Him, Krishna had to come. He protected her from enemies. Their tortures could not so much as touch her. He saved her when she was forced to drink poison and wear a venomous snake like a garland. Finally, He even took her to Vishnu-loka (the divine realm of Lord Vishnu) in body, a blessing bestowed very rarely in the history of humankind.

When Amma was a small child, Krishna would appear before Her whenever She called out to Him. She would dance with little Krishna every day. Finally, She revealed Her state of oneness with Krishna through Her Krishna Bhava. At the request of devotees, She transformed water into *panchamritam* (a consecrated sweet made from five ingredients) in the presence of non-believers and distributed it among thousands of people. Thus She demonstrated the greatness of devotion to others.

The poet sings,

> *Kaun kehte hain Bhagvan khaate nahin?*
> *Ber Sabari ke jaise khilaate nahin!*

> *Who says the Lord doesn't eat?*
> *You don't offer Him food like Sabari did!*

The humble Sabari was a great devotee of Sri Rama. When Sri Rama visited her modest hermitage, she offered him wild fruits that she had picked from the forest. But before offering them to the Lord, she made sure they were sweet by biting into each first! The Lord, moved by her innocent and pure love and devotion, heartily accepted her offering and ate it with great relish. The great devotee, drenched in the shower of divine love, washed Sri Rama's feet with tears of devotion and sanctified her human birth.

Sabari's story proves that the Lord accepts whatever we offer with pure love, be it even a half-eaten fruit! Hence, let us endeavour to perform all our actions with great love and await the shower of divine grace like Sabari did.

A few years ago, after the Brahmasthanam festival in Kochi, several devotees invited Amma to their homes. As darshan ended very late, Amma could not go. She consoled them by asking them to remind Her the next year. On Her way to the next programme venue, She visited a devotee's house that was close by. While there, Amma said that She wanted to speak to another devotee who had also invited Amma to her home, which was far away. I called her but her phone was switched off. Amma then said that She wanted to go to this devotee's house. Everyone told Her that it if She did so, She would reach the next programme venue very late. But Amma insisted.

Amma's convoy negotiated the busy roads and finally arrived at the devotee's house. All the doors were locked from the inside. We rang the bell and called out aloud, but there was no response. Finally, someone managed to enter the house somehow and found the devotee sitting and weeping in the puja room, oblivious to the goings on outside! She had been busy the entire previous night, preparing food for Amma and praying fervently for Her to accept the offering. Though Amma had not told her that She would visit, this devotee had told everyone that Amma would come! Hearing this, many people had laughed at her. It is said that the relatives of Poonthanam had also laughed at the great devotee when they saw him clean and decorate his house in anticipation of the Lord's arrival. He had had a dream in which the Lord had said that He was coming to take him. "What nonsense! The Lord coming to take you?" His friends and relatives had mocked. Poonthanam did not bother to reply, but waited with the Lord's name upon his lips. To the utter surprise and disbelief of everyone around, Poonthanam's mortal coil disappeared right before them in no time!

Even though Amma had not promised this devotee that She would visit, she somehow firmly believed that Amma would. That was why she had told everyone that Amma would come. When she heard that Amma was not coming, she had retired to the puja room to cry and pray, unable to bear the pain. Amma heard her prayer!

Amma let this devotee feed Her. The blessed devotee started feeding Amma, all the while chanting *"Om Amriteshwaryai Namah"* as tears streamed down her cheeks. Witnessing this scene reminiscent of the great devotee Sabari, many were moved to tears.

The poet further sings,

Kaun kehte hain Bhagvan sote nahin?
Maa Yashoda ke jaise sulaate nahin!

Who says the Lord doesn't come to sleep?
You don't put Him to sleep like mother Yashoda did!

To mother Yashoda, Lord Krishna was her child. She believed that He was her own. Not that she did not know that He was the Lord of the Universe. She had seen all the fourteen worlds in His little mouth. But she always loved to see Him as her little son. She lived each moment for her child. She caressed Him, fed Him, sang to Him, and put Him to sleep. All the while, she never sought from Him anything for herself.

We never allow the Lord to sleep. Most of us ruin His sleep by constantly placing our list of wants and litany of woes before Him. We often tell Amma, "O Amma, we feel very sad seeing You sit like this for hours, forgoing food and rest. You should sleep well. You should be careful about Your health. Please go and rest a bit, Amma!" And in just a few moments, we might tell Her, "Amma, may I ask You something? Why does everyone behave so cruelly with me? They are all so selfish and egoistic. Please punish them, Amma!" Even in Her divine presence, we see only the faults of others. This is not devotion. Devotion is seeing only the good in others.

The poet continues,

Kaun kehte hain Bhagvan naachte nahin?
Gopiyon ke jaise nachaate nahin!

Who says the Lord doesn't dance?
You don't make Him dance like the gopis did!

Everyone has heard of Lord Krishna's *Rasalila* dance. It was a beautiful moonlit night. The Lord decided it was the best time to fulfil His promise to the gopis of Vrindavan. They had been deeply desirous of dancing with Krishna. The Lord began to play heavenly music on His celestial flute, and the gopis dropped everything they were doing and rushed towards the source of the music.

Krishna was then just eleven years of age. Immersed in the dance, the gopis' awareness was single-pointed—they perceived Krishna and Krishna alone within and outside. They forgot everything else—their homes, husbands, children and parents. Their hearts melted in their love for Krishna and became one with Him. Melting in the crucible of devotion, their hearts merged in Him.

The gopis were no ordinary women. In the exalted state of devotion for Krishna, they become like yogis. Initially, Krishna nagged at and tried to dissuade them. "Why did you come here at this unearthly hour? Aren't you afraid of wild animals on the prowl at night? Don't you know it is not appropriate to be with other men at such hours?" He persuaded them to return to their homes.

Hearing these words, the gopis were distraught. They could not understand why Krishna seemed so heartless. They stood confused and sad, with heads lowered, and tearfully asked Krishna, "O Lord of our heart, why do You speak such cruel words? We have abandoned our worldly relationships and have come to offer ourselves to You, accepting You as the Lord of our lives. Please do not forsake us, Krishna!"

Their sorrow and deep devotion melted Krishna's heart. He sang and danced with them on the enchanting banks of the Yamuna. Miraculously, there was a Krishna for every gopi! As a result of this unearthly experience, their souls soared to the heights of samadhi.

We are blessed to witness Amma's divine dance every day. God is with us all the time, but we are unable to see Him with our senses. To transcend the senses and know God is not easy. Hence, God takes the form of a Guru. The Guru is the one who bestows liberation. We have the opportunity to establish a strong relationship of love, devotion and adoration with the Guru.

The Guru is not a person but a presence. It is through the Guru that the individual gets his very first experience of divinity. The Guru creates a *sadhak* (aspirant) out of the individual, transforms him and gives him a new life. As the seeker takes this journey through unknown and unfamiliar paths, leaving behind the darkness of ignorance and preparing to open the treasure troves of inner wisdom, he follows the Guru with complete faith. The Guru's blessing is an important factor. Through one's Guru, one gets an idea about one's future, about one's destiny. Just as a sapling bursts forth from the earth and grows towards the light, one grows through the Guru. One of the meanings of 'Guru' is 'that which has the power to attract'. The Guru exerts a kind of magnetic pull. In His presence, we feel we are being pulled towards His being.

The Guru is a strong magnet. However, we are not being pulled towards something external but towards our own inner divinity. Even as we gravitate towards the Guru, we become more and more self-reliant. Even as our surrender to the Guru deepens, we experience the solace and relief of real freedom, hitherto never experienced.

Amma says, "Children, make use of your wings as well as feet. Rise above and beyond the levels of body and mind. Spread your wings, transcend all limitations and soar high in the blissful skies of eternal freedom."

Through their lives, Avatars show us how to overcome life's challenges and rise to the highest state. This is what Amma is doing. May She bless us all to overcome all limitations and attain the highest state of God-realisation.

11

Bliss of Immortality

Man is seeking all his life. However, he does not know what he is seeking! Whatever he gains fails to give him contentment. From afar, everything appears beautiful. Seen from the earth, how splendid the moon looks! Poets sing of its beauty. However, should they set foot on the moon, they might be disappointed. Those who have gone to the moon say how much more beautiful the earth is! The most attractive object can become distasteful after some time. Whatever we procure becomes meaningless the moment we obtain it. Not being satisfied with whatever we have, we continue our search.

We live in this world with many selfish desires. We are not ready to share our blessings with others. If we are ready to share, more will come to us. Such is the law of nature. Is it possible to achieve total contentment and peace? "Yes," say mahatmas like Amma. However, in order to relish the beauty of life, we need to know certain secrets of life.

Life is like a movie in which God has given us a role to play. He is the director of the movie that is our life. He knows which role is most appropriate for us. We have already proven our histrionic skills through several old movies, i.e. our previous births. God has already seen them all. He has given us another chance to improve our acting. If He feels that we are not fit to don the human garb, He may give us the role of a bird or beast. Luckily, God has given us a human role. So, He expects more from us than from beasts and other beings.

We ought to manifest human qualities like compassion and forbearance. We must always wear a smiling face. Only humans can do it. Animals can cry, express anger and many other emotions but laugh they can't (except in cartoons!). They cannot enjoy jokes. It is only to human beings that God has given the faculty of discrimination. Now that we have obtained such a human birth, we must appreciate the significance of our role.

Where we were born or where we grew up is not all that important. We need not be anxious about the role we have been given either. Some get to play rich men, some, poor men. Still others may get the role of beggars. Whatever the role, God is constantly watching to see how we enact it: how we overcome obstacles and use our life to serve the world. We can prove our capabilities better in adversity.

If we are rich, we can play our role well by helping the poor. By God's grace, even a beggar can become an emperor. Even if a movie were ordinary, the actor playing the beggar can win an Oscar. The only consideration for the award would be how well he played the role.

Whether we are rich or poor is not important. God looks only at how we use our capabilities to overcome the challenges of life and contribute to this world. However, if we keep repeating the same mistakes over and over again, the director will have to demonstrate how to play the part to perfection. He will then don the human role and act. Such directors are Avatars. Amma reveals this through Her life.

Born into the midst of difficulties, Amma nevertheless rose above them. She was born in a coastal village among poor people. Though there was none to show Her love or sympathy, She was able to awaken Her divine nature and create a paradise around Herself, a moving paradise! In the ecstasy of supreme bliss that Her divine presence creates, thousands of people forget their sorrows.

I am reminded of Amma's maiden visit to Dubai. The flight was from Kochi Airport. Thousands of devotees were waiting outside to see Her, and the police found it difficult to control the crowd. We thought, after entering the airport, She will be able to rest in the VIP lounge. But all the airport employees and officers came there for Her darshan. That over, following the security check, we moved into the restricted area, where the security officers arrived for darshan. I thought that at least after boarding the plane, Amma might be able to rest a couple of hours.

She boarded the plane first. When the other passengers boarded the plane, they learnt that Amma was on board. Everyone became eager to get darshan without tokens! Elsewhere, they would have to wait a long time even to obtain tokens. Even those who had no belief in God wanted to have Amma's darshan. The passengers got up and started moving towards Amma. Seeing the crowd, the cabin crew became anxious. They announced that all passengers should return to their seats for the take-off. But who could forgo a golden chance to be with Amma? At last, the pilot himself promised that everyone would be given an opportunity to go for darshan once the flight was airborne. Only then did the passengers return to their seats.

The flight took off. In a short while, the passengers experienced the truth that they were transcending the dark clouds of sorrows and being uplifted to the infinite skies of endless peace. The airline staff permitted the passengers to approach Amma one by one. They themselves helped the passengers. Seat numbers became token numbers. By then, a few devotees seated near Amma began to sing bhajans. Some swayed to the rhythm of the songs. The aircraft became like a temple. People even forgot that they were on a plane! The flight attendants, too, came for darshan. They kept bringing juices, coffee and other goodies so that Amma would look at them again and again. Finally, the pilot and co-pilots also came for darshan one after the other. Luckily, they did not come together!

What is the reason for this attraction for Amma? That is the beauty of Perfection. Amma creates heaven around Her wherever

She travels. She spreads the fragrance of love all around. It is this Perfection that we are all seeking. Only through spirituality can we experience the beauty of that Perfection. For that we need to know how we can enact our role beautifully.

This body is a gift from God. We must honour it and not misuse it through drugs and other intoxicants. The food we eat must be pure, remembering that it is an offering to the divine enshrined within. We have no right to dishonour our body. We should always keep it pure and healthy. Amma often says that the body is a rented house. A tenant renting a house cannot do as he pleases. He will need to vacate it sooner or later, and ensure that the house is in good condition. Similarly, we need to return this body to God. It is His temple. A temple transmits peace around. So also, we must be able to transmit peace around us. We must respect other bodies as well. We must behold every object in this world with reverence. Only then can we relish divine beauty. Mahatmas know that they are only acting. Therefore, suffering does not touch them. Not so with us. We get identified with our roles. Mahatmas use their body but never identify with it.

Amma does not feel that She is confined to any one body. She is aware that all bodies are Hers. Therefore, She is not anxious about losing a body. Amma can cast away Her body with the same ease with which one would a garment.

God is always with us but we are unable to know Him with our senses. To know God, we need to transcend the plane of the senses. This is not easy for the ordinary man. That is why God has to take a form perceptible to the five senses. That is Incarnation or Avatar, which means the descent of God. God comes down as a Guru. Through the example of Her own life, Amma is trying to teach us how to overcome the difficulties of life.

12

The Great Ritual Called Life

Our life should become a yajna, an offering to God. How can we do so? In Amma's words, there is no action that cannot be rendered spiritual. We must be able to convert all actions into a yajna. That is what Lord Sri Krishna advised Arjuna in the battlefield of Kurukshetra: how even a war can be transformed into a yajna. We read in the *Puranas* that King Daksha's yajna was transformed into a battle. But Arjuna's battle became a yajna. The attitude with which one performs an action is more important that the action itself.

Sage Vasishtha told Sri Rama:

Manah kritam kritam Rama
Na shareera kritam kritam

The mind does everything, Rama.
The body does not do anything.

If we know how to act only with the body, our action will not attract karmic consequences. But all our actions are backed by the mind. Many a time, we do the *archana* (floral worship) or puja with our bodies, but if our minds are elsewhere, our worship amounts to mere physical exercise. So only what is done with the mind is true action, and not what we have done with our body. Even if we have not done anything physically, if we have done it mentally, we will obtain its fruit. Many lament, "O God, I have done no wrong so far in this life. Why, then, do I have to suffer so?" True, they may not have done anything wrong physically but they would have, mentally. For in the eyes of nature, everything is karma. Whatever is done—whether physically, verbally or mentally—is karma, which has its consequences.

Long ago, there was a time when I would ask Amma many questions. Once I told Her, "Amma, I'm so angry with God that I could kill Him!"

"Why?" She asked.

"In this world, some suffer from disease, poverty and sorrows while others bask in affluence. In nature, every being has been created as food for another being. If there's a God who created such a cruel world, I'm angry with that God."

Amma said, "Amma likes you, son, for your anger does not stem from selfishness but from compassion for others. God dwells in the heart that is compassionate to others. God's nature is love. He is an embodiment of compassion. God can never punish. He knows only how to save. Therefore, what appears as punishment in this world is not so. They are only the reactions of nature. Having hurled stones upward, how can we expect a shower of flowers in return?"

This was what the wife of Ratnakara, the dreaded jungle dacoit, advised him aeons ago. She played the role of a Guru in his life. "One who does karma must experience the result thereof." One cannot share the result with others but must experience it oneself. Certain incidents in our life will unveil the mysteries of karma. There is no use blaming God. Nature follows certain laws. It does not know compassion. Whether a child, scholar or pious soul jumps from a building, the same law of nature will work. Those who use the faculty of discernment that God has given man, those who know how to turn the laws of nature to their advantage, will be able to avoid calamities.

The great masters exhort us to live according to the principles of dharma. Many of the sorrows we undergo in our lives are not God's creations but man's.

The sun does not create darkness. How can one ask the sun, "Why did you create darkness on one side of the earth?"

The sun would reply, "Darkness? What's that?"

There is no darkness in the sun's world. The sun is one who dispels darkness. If the sun asked us where darkness is, we might say, "Come, let me show you. Darkness is on the other side of the earth."

But if you orbit the earth with the sun, would you be able to show darkness to the sun? No! Similarly, there are no sorrows in God's world. The instant we behold God, the embodiment of bliss, our sorrows vanish. We will understand this if we observe the people coming to Amma. Most people cry like small children when they come to Her. If you ask them why they are crying, they will not be able to answer. Usually, we need a reason to cry. But there are times when we cry for no reason. This happens all the time in Amma's presence. When do we cry? When the ego disappears. Usually, the ego only recedes when one feels intense sorrow. A child can cry anytime or anywhere because it has no ego. Crying is the only language it knows. Similarly, at the sight or touch of a mahatma, the iceberg of our ego may melt down and flow as tears. On such occasions, we can obtain God's grace in abundance.

The sorrows in this tangible world are not God's handiwork but the consequences of man's karma alone. We have also the strength to change them. If fate is the fruit of karma, then God has endowed us with the strength to alter fate. It is only after giving us the strength to surmount all sorrows that God has given us this human birth. Not understanding this, some falter. This was the case with Arjuna in the *Mahabharata*.

The Mahabharata War is not an event that happened only in Kurukshetra many years ago. It is an incessant war going on within us. When we falter and stumble in the face of insignificant sorrows, we must recall the *Bhagavad Gita*. This is what Gurus are teaching us again and again. There is no need to panic seeing the sorrows in the world. Nature has already given us the strength to surmount them. Those who know how to use it emerge victorious; others fail. We must learn the great secret that Lord Krishna breathed into a crestfallen Arjuna's ears on the battlefield of Kurukshtera.

Once, a professor rushed to a student who had fainted in the examination hall, sprinkled water on his face, and roused the student. When the student came to, the professor asked him, "What happened?"

The student said, "I had studied everything but can't remember anything!"

The Professor whispered something into his ears. Hearing it, the student sprang up and started writing the answers to the examination question. He went on to score the highest marks! What was the secret that the Professor whispered? The same secret that Krishna whispered in Arjuna's ears long ago to spur him into action. The great warrior Arjuna, the invincible Arjuna, the war-hungry Arjuna had lost all confidence. The *gandiva* (Arjuna's mighty bow) slipped from his hands. That was when Krishna whispered the secret in his ears: "Arjuna, you are a mighty warrior. You needn't be afraid at all. My *sudarshana-chakra* (Krishna's disk-like weapon) alone is enough to vanquish the entire Kaurava force. You only need to shoot your arrow. I will manage the rest!" Thus, the Lord inspired Arjuna who had collapsed from despondency.

So also, the professor told the student, "Child, I know that you're a good student. It is I who will be evaluating your paper.

You needn't worry at all. Whatever you write, I shall award you full marks!"

Instantly, the student regained confidence and was able to write the answers. The professor did not have to give him marks for nothing. His confidence restored his memory and he was able to answer all the questions correctly.

We need teachers who can instil confidence in us. Normally, the experiences in the world disillusion us. The world seems blind to our virtues and feeds only our weaknesses. We need a Guru to awaken the good in us. The Guru is pure enough to see only the good in us. Only the Guru, who knows the infinite potential in us, can awaken the divine latent in us. Only then can we transform every moment in the battlefield of life into a celebration. Therefore, worldly education alone will not be enough for us to enjoy life.

This was also what the Greek philosopher reclining half-naked on the riverbank told Alexander, the Great long ago. Seeing Alexander pass by, the philosopher asked, "Where are you going in such a hurry?"

"To conquer the world."

Hearing Alexander's reply, the philosopher smiled and asked him, "What after that?"

The Emperor had no answer! He remained silent for some time and then said, "I will enjoy some rest after that."

The philosopher said, "Look here. Don't you see me resting, enjoying the cool of this river, breathing in the beauty of the clear blue sky, and adoring the caressing breeze? If you want to rest, come and join me. You can rest right now. Can't you see that I am resting even without conquering the world?"

Alexander replied, "No, I cannot rest until I have conquered the world, so strong is my desire for conquest! I shall return here after conquering the world and join you then."

The philosopher then said something very profound, something worthy of careful attention. It is something Amma tells us often: "Children, if you want to do something good, do it right now!" The philosopher told Alexander the same thing: "If you want to do something, do it right now. Tomorrow might turn out to be an unreality!"

But, paying no heed to it, Alexander marched towards India. In the war that ensued, two thirds of his army was vanquished. He suffered a fatal injury. When death was certain, he reportedly told his companions, "Upon my death, let my body be placed in a coffin with an opening each on both sides through which both my hands will stick out. Let my coffin be carried in a procession."

They asked him, "Why this strange kind of coffin?"

Alexander said, "It must tell the world that Alexander, who wished to conquer the world, is going away empty-handed, taking nothing with him! Nobody should repeat my mistake. That is why I want it so."

As the procession of mourners carrying the coffin passed the philosopher, he smiled and muttered, "A hearse for him who yearned to conquer the world!"

In a sense, all of us are Alexanders yearning to conquer the world. The ordinary man feels he has conquered the world when wealth, fame and fortune come. We are ready to endure any amount of hardship because of this urge to conquer the world. But a time will come when our intellect, might and talents fail us in the face of life's experiences. Our only refuge then will be our virtuous actions.

Is it possible to conquer the world? Amma says that it is indeed possible with divine love! She is demonstrating to us that where weapons fail, divine love wins. In Her life, we witness the great miracle of the world being conquered by love. Amma teaches us how to enjoy the comfort of relaxation even while performing actions. Actions performed with love impart the bliss of relaxation.

What makes life beautiful is not intelligence or material gains. It is the purity required to grow into the realms of intuitive experience. If we succeed in attaining that purity, our life will be transformed into a yajna.

13

The Five Great Secrets of Success

It is true that modern man lives in the midst of complicated problems. Nevertheless, he can still surmount all obstacles and transform life into a divine experience. For those who live by the laws of nature, i.e. abide by dharma, nature will protect them from sorrowful experiences.

We have come to this world to exhaust our karmic baggage through various kinds of experiences, and thereby uncover our divine nature. Different people have various experiences in life. But if we lack the strength to face adversities, we will succumb in critical situations. When experience weakens us, we lose our confidence and experience untold misery. We see this even in developed countries.

No matter where in the world we go, we will see all kinds of people suffering from sorrow; the only difference will be the reasons for their sorrows. Some experience sorrow because of poverty, others because of affluence. But the sorrow of those who have and those who do not is alike. Those with jobs and those without jobs, those with children and those without—all have their share of sorrows. Both the haves and have-nots experience sorrow. Only one who knows how to awaken one's spiritual energy can enjoy life. Ordinarily, in the rush of life, people are not aware of valuable moments ebbing away. Mahatmas reiterate that life is invaluable and that the human body is special. We must know how to use it in the right manner. If we know how to do so, what awaits us is nothing less than Godhood itself! God does not want to give us anything less than that. He has no difficulty answering our small prayers and satisfying our small desires. But we should not conclude from this that God can bestow on us only such trivial things.

Let us not make the mistake of asking a benevolent king, who is ever ready to give us anything we want, for a pumpkin! Of course we can ask God to ease our sufferings or to fulfil our desires, but we must strive to gain what matters from God. If He appeared before us and asked us to request for just one boon, what would we ask for? Tricky! Desires being many, which one will we choose to fulfil? The ideal devotee would pray that God be with him always. Just as sunlight dispels darkness, the light of knowledge dispels the darkness of sorrow and suffering. In short, by attaining God, one attains everything.

So there is no need to wander here and there in search of solutions to our sorrows. All that we need to do is to transform ourselves in such a way that we can feel God's presence constantly. Many ask, what is the need or relevance of worship and prayer? God does not need our worship and prayer. Through worship, we can awaken the divine power inherent in us and nourish our divine qualities. To attain God, there is only one prerequisite: purity. Whatever 'qualifications' we have might, in fact, disqualify us from attaining Him. When we purify ourselves, we will experience the all-pervading nature of God. Such a person will be fearless.

Krishna inspired a despondent Arjuna during the Kurukshetra War. He told him that there was no need to lose heart in a crisis. The Lord assured him that it was possible to overcome all obstacles and attain victory in this war field of life. When God is with us, we need not fear anything. But this world has been designed in such a manner that only those who live in accordance with dharma can find happiness. The cosmos has a flow. For one who knows how to go with the flow, life is effortless. Most people move against the tide; they are the ones who violate the laws of nature. There will be no end to problems for them. Spirituality teaches us how to live in accordance with the laws of nature. Our worship traditions are all such as harmonise us with nature's laws. Our acharyas did not talk about a God in the skies. He is the effulgence immanent in all that is sentient and insentient in the world. It permeates and surrounds us.

Ask the spiritual masters about God, and they will say He is omnipresent and omnipotent. If God is omnipresent, there is nowhere He is not. He is present in stone and thorn, flower and tree, bird and beast, as well as human beings. As divine energy permeates everything, we can awaken that power in anything. Thus we can invoke divinity within ourselves, in a rock or a tree.

God is omnipotent. We need not vex ourselves trying to decide if He is formless or with form. Omnipotence encompasses all capabilities. The omnipotent one is capable of anything. So if one likes to conceive of God as someone with form, He will have no difficulty in assuming that form. What is important is not what others have told us, but our own concept or sankalpa. God can appear in the form of our pure sankalpa. Some conceive of God without form, name and qualities, or God without attributes. God can bestow such experiences, too. Yet others conceived of God as having a maternal nature. To some, God is remover of obstacles, and to others, the Goddess of Knowledge. God manifests in accordance with one's sankalpa. We regard His various manifestations as deities.

Some feel that there is no God. To them, God appears as if He is not! Thus, God is the miraculous power we experience according to our personal sankalpa.

Water flows in the river. One who sits on the riverbank and thinks, "I'm not going to believe in this river. This is not water!" could die of thirst! The river is ready to give water and purify us. It welcomes one who enters it. Likewise, we are living in the ocean of divine effulgence. The vast majority of people are like fish in an aquarium. The fish never thinks of the water or even knows that it is in water. But when it is caught and thrown on land, it will think of water for the first time in its life. Writhing and wriggling, it will long to get back into water. Similarly, so long as we have good health and good fortune, we are unlikely to think of God. However, in a crisis, when we are helpless, we will cry out to God. Often, this happens too late. Sometimes, discernment dawns only on the deathbed! It is then that surrender arises. Those who strive to know God and to awaken their divine potential while they enjoy good health and fortune will not have to suffer the pains and pangs of life. God Himself will see to it that such a person is protected from misery. Nature protects those who live in such a way as to bring good to others. Therefore, the acharyas insist that we must perform five kinds of yajnas in life.

Deva Yajna

We want to be successful in whatever we do. However, human effort alone is not enough; to succeed, we need God's grace also. Therefore, after our morning bath, let us first do some spiritual practices before going about our daily business. Praying at dawn and dusk is our dharma. Just as an electronic gadget needs to be charged first before operating it, we need to charge our body and mind with practices like mantra chanting and meditation. Morning prayers help us assimilate divine energy. We will then find that the actions performed later will not be too strenuous. Those actions will meet with success. At dusk, negative vibrations fill the air. They will affect us if we engage in any activity other than prayer then. Earlier on, family members would gather to sit and pray together. As the very air is impure then, those engaged in work other than prayer will be susceptible to disease. If we are not home at dusk, we should at least chant our mantra.

Today, in most homes, people watch soap operas on television then and shed tears! How much more beneficial it would be to shed tears of devotion chanting names of God! Amma says, "People shed buckets of tears for worldly matters. If only we can shed a single tear for God, we won't have to shed buckets of tears." Prayer is a must at twilight. Prayers at dawn and dusk are an offering to the devas. They rush to the homes where there is prayer, as prayer is food for them. Homes that devatas visit will always be prosperous. The Goddess of Auspiciousness is sure to bless such homes.

Rishi Yajna

We have certain obligations to the rishis, who gave us the knowledge of how to enjoy happiness while alive and even after death. We would do well to become well-versed with the principles expounded in the *Bhagavad Gita*. Importantly, we must impart those principles to our children. These principles, which the rishis expounded, teach us how to face and overcome the challenges of life. Sharing it with others is our dharma and our obligation to the rishis.

Pitru Yajna

We are able to enjoy many good things today because of our ancestors' efforts. We are thus obliged to them. We must honour and respect the elders at home. Today, many of the elders are abandoned, whereas grandchildren used to regard their grandparents dearly in the past. Now, computers and mobile phones have made grandparents unnecessary!

Once, the parents of a child who was being relocated to India visited me. I asked them, "Why are you separating your child from you?" They told me that the child's grandparents were here in India and that it was difficult to look after them well abroad. I asked the seven-year-old girl, "Daughter, won't you find it difficult to live away from your parents?"

She said, "Nothing like that, Swami. There's always the computer, isn't there?"

Gadgets have become dearer to children than their own parents. So, even the bond between parents and children has begun to weaken. We must teach children to treat elders with respect. Respecting and looking after elders and making them happy are part of Pitru Yajna.

Nara Yajna

Millions of people in this world do not enjoy many of fortunes we have—the blind, the deaf, the lame, the mute, and those who need the help of machines even to breathe! We should take care of such people; such is the law of nature. Compassion towards fellow human beings is Nara Yajna.

Bhuta Yajna

We need the blessings of everyone in this world to live peacefully, even that of an ant! An ant could spoil our moments of happiness. Plants and animals contribute to making this world a beautiful place. If trees disappeared, man would die for want of oxygen. If bees and butterflies disappeared, pollination will not take place and man will suffer without food. If we do not conserve nature, man will not be able to live here peacefully. Without plants, birds and animals, the rhythm and harmony of the earth will be lost. Hence, the acharyas advise us to treat all forms of life with reverence. Birds and animals, too, have a right to live here. So, if you can satisfy yourself with a vegetarian diet, please leave them alone.

Upon the successful completion of ten thousand heart surgeries at the AIMS hospital, a team of scientists undertook a survey to study the food habits of the patients who had undergone the surgeries. Their report was shocking. A large majority of the patients were non-vegetarians, who consumed meat excessively. It is our dharma to keep our body pure. Therefore, we should consume pure food and drinks. As the body is a temple of God, whatever we eat or drink is an offering to the indwelling divinity. If we wish to be happy in this world, we first need the blessings of our own body. If we do not look after our body, we may suffer endless woes later. Therefore, we must maintain its health and retain its purity. We can perform good deeds only through the body, and thus obtain God's blessings. The body is God's gift. We have no right to torture it. We must not do anything that disgraces it. Likewise, as other bodies are also temples, we must regard them also with reverence. Similarly, as God dwells in all kinds of life forms, we must regard them all with reverence. Amma says that if we claim to believe in God, we must learn to revere the divinity that inheres in everyone and everything, sentient and insentient.

God is not a being who dwells in a particular place alone but the Power that is immanent in creation. A true devotee venerates everything in creation. Some people complain that despite believing in God, they suffer. Which God do they believe in? One who dwells in everything? A true believer reveres everything. Nature will specially protect such a person.

Amma often says that prayer or worship is not an activity we do sitting in a fixed place alone. A smiling face is prayer. A word of consolation is prayer. All that brings good to others are prayers. Selfless actions born of love are prayers. God is the great fortune that only people who have made their entire life a prayer obtain.

Some ask Amma if there is an easy way to earn God's blessings. The shortcut is sacrifice. Amma says, "The easiest way to earn God's grace is through renunciation, self-sacrifice." Only through sacrifice can one earn God's blessings. The scriptures declare, *'Tyagenaike amritatvamanasu'* ('Immortality is achieved through sacrifice alone'). Without sacrifice, one can never attain God. God is a great fortune that only selfless people can obtain. That is why Amma incarnated as the epitome of sacrifice.

14

Divine Magic

A t least some people wonder, why worship God? God does not gain anything from our devotion or worship. Faith in God awakens divine qualities in us. It uplifts us from the human plane to the divine. However, man has kept God at bay, far away in the skies, beyond the stellar realms. But the rishis of Bharat proclaimed to the world for the first time, "God is not far away but within us." What is hidden in our heart? What is hidden in our inhalation and exhalation? What is our true nature? Divinity. God is all-pervading, and therefore in us, too. Why then do we not experience Him? What veils God? Or rather, can God be veiled? Can a tiny cloud conceal the sun? Never. But the clouds of our ego *appear* to eclipse God. Some people say that they could not find God after searching for Him everywhere. This is like saying, "I looked everywhere in the piano and even removed its parts, but still failed to find music within. So there is nothing called music." Just as music is hidden in the piano, God is hidden everywhere in the universe. Worship helps us discover Him.

Amma says, "There is air everywhere; it could be still, waft gently as a breeze, blow as a wind, rage as a tempest, or become a tornado. Likewise, divine power is immanent; it can remain unknown, be known a little, or experienced in its entirety." Temples enable the ordinary person to experience divinity. Amma says that external temples help us become mobile temples ourselves eventually. As God is omnipresent, He is present even in stone. There is nowhere that God is not. It is in the form of cosmic energy, the animating power, and effulgence. There is energy everywhere. Scientists say that the universe is a flow of energy. The rishis say that the basis of the universe is the dance of Nataraja, the Master Dancer. This is just a difference in terminology.

Energy flow and the dance of divine effulgence—both are the same. God, which pervades everything as energy flow, resides in us, too. He has no form or name. However, Amma says that all names and forms belong to God. He is capable of assuming a form in accordance with the devotee's wish. Though ocean water has no form, in extreme cold, it takes the form of ice. Likewise, at the 'extreme cold' of devotion ecstasy in the devotee, the formless God assumes a form. That is the concept behind Avatars.

Good thoughts and deeds eliminate sorrows from life. Good thoughts and good actions help usher in prosperity. Rituals give us the initial training to cultivate good thoughts.

God is not a person but a position, just as a president is a position. Anyone can hold that position. However, to hold that office, the candidate needs people's votes. So also, to attain the Godhead, we need the blessings of all that is sentient and insentient. Anyone can attain God. Worshipping God is the means to attain that state of perfection.

What sustains this earth, its oceans, and the glorious lives that sprout and flourish here is the purity of human actions. The thoughts and deeds of humans are reflected everywhere on earth. God has created an immensely beautiful world, but it is not separate from Him. In this splendid creation, human minds sow toxic seeds. So, by purifying the mind, we can sanctify the world. To bring about phenomenal changes in life, we need both outer and inner purity. Lord Krishna's advice to Arjuna in the *Bhagavad Gita* was not just an exhortation to fight. Fighting implies at least two. When one gains the non-dualistic experience that there is only oneself in the Universe, one realizes there is no 'other' with whom to fight. Or rather, when one can love others as oneself, wars end. In Bharat, all modes of worship train us to attain that supreme experience of non-duality.

Years ago, when the *Atiratram* (an elaborate Vedic ritual) was performed in north Kerala, a large number of foreign scientists came to study the phenomenon. They brought with them instruments to study the changes that yajnas bring about in nature. These instruments started detecting the strong presence of gamma rays in the hall where the yajna was performed. The scientists were wonderstruck! How can gamma rays arise from a sacrificial pit? Later, they asked the priests, who speculated that the rays were from the *darbha* grass (a tropical grass considered sacred in Vedic scriptures). Later, the scientists tested this hypothesis and found it to be true. What baffled them, however, was how these priests who were not conversant with modern science knew this.

The rishis say that the *Kali Yuga* (the Dark Age of Materialism, the present age) is most conducive for attaining God. When faced with adversity, man realises the limitations of his intellect. Sorrows alone kill his ego and inspire him to turn Godward. If we succeed in directing our sorrows to God, we will experience these very sorrows being transmuted into blessings. That is why Amma says that we need not fear conflicts or disturbances. Just as night disappears at dawn, the darkness of delusion flees when knowledge dawns.

15

Amritavarshini

Amma's children have seen divine qualities manifest in Her countless times. Her invisible presence has saved devotees from dangers untold number of times! Once, actor and singer Krishnachandran witnessed one such experience. What drove him and his wife Vanitha to Amma was the sorrow of not having a child even after two years of marriage. When they first met Amma in Chennai on February 27, 1988, they wept uncontrollably. They were not sure if it was the sorrow of childlessness or the overwhelming elation at having met their Sadguru that made them cry! Amma gave them a banana that She blessed, and told them to have unshakeable faith in the Supreme even if they were not destined to have a child. After eating this banana, Vanitha conceived. Amma named their daughter Amritavarshini. When Amma's life story was televised, Amritavarshini was blessed with the opportunity to play the role of little Krishna.

In January 1990, before he returned from a devotees' camp in Amritapuri, Amma whispered into Krishnachandran's ear, "It won't take long, son!" Vanitha became pregnant soon thereafter. At each stage of pregnancy, they went to receive Amma's blessings. According to the doctor, the date of delivery was October 30, 1990. In those days, Amma's birthday used to be celebrated according to the Malayalam calendar, and it was to fall on October 7 that year. Krishnachandran had arranged a devotional music programme by singers from Chennai. The programme went off very well on the 7th. Amma called all the singers to Her room and gave them darshan and a gold ring each. Krishnachandran alone did not receive anything from Her. He felt sad.

The next day, Amma called him to Her room. She said, "I did not give you anything!" She then removed one of Her *rudraksha* bracelets (bracelets made of seeds from the Elaeocarpus tree) and gave it to him. Only later did he understand that that was the beginning of a series of events that would completely transform their lives! He realised that the bracelet Amma gave him was a protective armour.

He returned to Chennai on October 10 and gave Vanitha the prasad that Amma had sent for her. Even though the delivery was due for the 30th of the month, Vanitha surprised even her doctor by delivering a girl child at two o'clock that very afternoon.

Two days after the child was born, a friend informed Krishnachandran that the doors to their house were open. On reaching home, he saw that the house had been burgled. Everything had been stolen! The thieves had taken even the awards and medals that Krishnachandran had won from his school days. Even their puja room had been ransacked. Needless to say, he was terribly upset. The police were called. They noted down the things that had been stolen and then left.

What upset Krishnachandran most was that the sari that Amma had blessed and Her photograph, both of which had been kept in the puja room, had been stolen! When Amma visited his home, Krishnachandran and Vanitha had performed *pada puja* (ceremonial worship of the Guru's Feet) and draped a sari around Her as an offering. Amma had blessed and returned the sari to them. They had carefully wrapped it in silk and placed it in the puja room. A photograph of Amma had been placed on it.

With tear-filled eyes, Krishnachandran prayed fervently to Amma to restore the sari at least. He asked several people, including his neighbours, but no one knew anything about the burglary. Broken-hearted, he called Amritapuri. Amma told him, "Don't worry, son, nothing has been lost. You will get everything back!"

The very next day, he received a message from the police station asking him to report there. After asked him in detail about all the stolen articles, the inspector took him to a room in which the stolen articles were stored. Krishnachandran stood stunned! Every single stolen item was there, including Amma's sari!

It was the sari that had proved to be the thief's undoing. The policemen explained how. The robbery had taken place at two o'clock at night when no one was home. The thief loaded all the goods into an auto-rickshaw and sped along the streets of Chennai, avoiding the main roads. Suddenly, he saw a woman clad in white standing right in the middle of the road. He applied the brakes. The vehicle lost control, rammed against an electric post, and overturned. All the stolen goods were scattered on the road. Policemen who were on night patrol stopped their vehicle and questioned the driver, who said that he was shifting house and transferring his things to the new home. The policemen helped him pick up the scattered items. One of them noticed Amma's sari lying on the road. When he picked it up, a photo-graph fell from its folds. He noticed the thief start on seeing the photograph. The policeman examined it and asked the thief who it was. Not knowing what to say, the thief began to hum and haw. It was Amma's photograph! One of the policemen who had been on duty during the Chennai Brahmasthanam festival instantly recognised Amma. The thief finally admitted that he had stolen the items.

Krishnachandran had not understood why Amma had returned the sari to them, when it had been intended as an offering to Her. Nevertheless, obeying Her instructions, he had kept it in the puja room along with the picture. It was this picture that helped the policemen find the thief, who confessed to his crime. Yet the police could not believe the thief when he said that a woman clad in white had been standing in the middle of the road. When asked if he had recognised the woman, the thief trembled and said it was the lady in the picture! His words silenced the police. Of course, Krishnachandran had no doubt that it was Amma!

What further proof do we need to understand how lovingly Amma protects those who have dedicated their lives to Her? Krishnachandran has had many unbelievable experiences with Amma. This particular incident deepened his faith and devotion, and was the beginning of a life of even deeper surrender. Later, the family relocated to Kerala and became involved with Amrita Television. With Amma's blessings, today, Krishnachandran is in charge of the musical programmes in Amrita Television.

16

How to Conquer Fear

Everything on earth is fraught with fear. Only one who has renounced everything can be fearless. Fear is not something that affects just an individual or a community. It engulfs the whole world. We are all slaves to fear of one kind or another, and are trying to overcome these fears.

What is the root cause of all fear? The great rishis found the answer to this riddle aeons ago. As long as man is identified with his body, freedom from fear is impossible; it can only be reduced to some extent. The ultimate solution to fear is to know one's Self, i.e. attain Self-realisation.

Bhartruhari, the great poet-seer of ancient India, observed that there were nine kinds of fear. A momentous incident that occurred in his life completely transformed his perception of the world. A king, he renounced everything and became a monk.

A great sage once visited King Bhartruhari's court. The king at once got up from the throne, prostrated at the sage's feet and engaged in his service. Pleased with the king's devotion and humility, the sage gave him a special fruit that bestowed longevity.

Bhartruhari was married to a charming queen whom he loved dearly. He felt she deserved the fruit the most and so gave it to her. The queen had a charioteer who used to take her around the kingdom, and she was in love with him. Wanting him to live long, she gave him the fruit.

The charioteer was in love with a prostitute. He gave her the fruit because he wanted her to live long. The prostitute, however, thought, "Of what use is a long life to me? It will only serve to bring about the downfall of many people. There is no use in prolonging my sinful life. We have a noble king, who is looking after the welfare of the land and its people in all earnestness. It is he who deserves this fruit and who ought to live a long life!"

Thus the fruit found its way back into the king's hands. Coming to know of the whole story, the king was shocked beyond words! He instantly felt deep dispassion. He thought, "No one truly loves anyone in this world. There is no one to call one's own!" This truth sank deep in his mind. He felt detached from the fickle world and its fleeting pleasures. Renouncing his kingdom, he set off for the forest to lead a life of austerities. He spent many years practising severe penance and meditation, and finally attained enlightenment. Thereafter, he wrote a treatise called *Vairagya Shatakam*. The thirty-first verse from this treatise reads thus:

Bhoge roga bhayam kule chyuti bhayam
Vitte nripaalaat bhayam
Maane dainya bhayam bale ripu bhayam
Roope jaraayaa bhayam

Seekers of pleasure fear disease. The high born fear a fall.
The wealthy fear authority.
The proud fear humiliation. The powerful fear adversaries.
The beautiful are wary of old age.

Shaastre vaadi bhayam gune khala bhayam
Kaaye kritaantaat bhayam
Sarvam vastu bhayaanvitam bhuvi
Nrinaam vairagyameva abhayam.

The erudite fear learned scholars. The virtuous fear the wicked.
The body fears death.
Everything in the world is fraught with fear.
Vairagya, dispassion, alone bestows fearlessness.

1. **'Bhoge roga bhayam'**—Those who revel in sense pleasures fear disease. They live in constant fear of their enjoyments coming to an end one day. We need the blessing of our body to enjoy life. If the body is ailing, we cannot enjoy life. The mere thought of serious disease is enough to rob us of happiness and peace of mind. Even though we may have wealth, power and influence, we must accept that we can fall ill some day.

2. **'Kule chyuti bhayam'**—Wherever there is pride in ancestry, there is also the fear of social decline. This fear remains even if the person has health, wealth, power and influence. He will be tormented by thoughts about his children and grandchildren, and their safety and well-being. He will be anxious about the reputation of his family, and worry if future generations might bring disrepute to the family.

3. **'Vitte nripaalaat bhayam'**—Where there is wealth, there is fear of authority. If one has a lot of wealth, one must submit records and pay taxes. There is also the fear of losing the wealth, which is tied to one's sense of security. At first, one is preoccupied with amassing wealth. Then one becomes anxious about safeguarding it. Finally, one fears losing it. Thus wealth, too, becomes a source of fear.

4. **'Maane dainya bhayam'**—The proud one fears humiliation or ignominy. Used to respect, humiliation might seem worse than death even. All of us want recognition, praise, respect and acceptance from others, but mahatmas like Amma are not like that. Praise them, and they are happy. Insult them, they are happier! Nobody can humiliate or insult Amma because She has no ego. Where there is no 'I' sense, there can be no experience of humiliation. But ordinary people are often tormented by thoughts of losing respect. They find it hard to accept insult or humiliation with equanimity.

5. **'Bale ripu bhayam'**—The strong live in constant fear of enemies. If one's power arises from wealth and position, then one will fear someone of greater wealth and position. Thus powerful people, too, live in fear.

6. **'Roope jaraayaam bhayam'**—Those who are proud of their physical beauty fear losing it. They want their physical charm to remain intact forever. But this cannot be as the body changes every minute and dies bit by bit every day. Therefore, the fear of change and old age is very real.

7. **'Shaastre vaadi bhayam'**—The learned also live in fear. In ancient times, scholars used to engage in debates and take pride in defeating their opponents. They feared more learned opponents. When someone attends a job interview, he fears smarter people or those with higher qualifications landing the job. Thus, even learning leads to fear.

8. **'Gune khala bhayam'**—The virtuous are afraid of the wicked. They fear that keeping the company of the wicked might rob them of their own goodness or that the wicked might harm them. Many consider themselves more virtuous than others, leading to the fear that others might bring about their downfall. Amma says that our presence should bring peace to others, just as a temple does. When the body and mind become pure like a temple, our being will radiate peace. We will be transformed into moving temples. Amma is a living example of this. She is able to confer peace on millions of people all over the world. We must aim to transform ourselves in such a way that our mere presence can bring about a transformation in others.

9. **'Kaaye kritaantaat bhayam'**—The greatest fear is the fear of death. Everyone lives in mortal fear of Kala, the God of Death. Kala also implies time. Time or death conquers even the

most arrogant person. All arrogance crumbles at the moment of death.

Everything on the face of this earth can induce fear. Vairagya, or non-attachment to the things of the world, alone can liberate us from fear.

Amma says that one's life can be compared to the various stages of the day. Dawn is extremely beautiful. The sun rises, the birds sing, flowers bloom, purity abounds. Similarly, childhood is the most attractive phase of life. The innate purity and innocence of children make childhood very beautiful.

The sun is strongest at noontime. Similarly, youth is the period of life when one has most enthusiasm, energy, strength and vitality. It is the period when one longs to apply one's knowledge, talent and capabilities in various areas of expertise. This strength and vitality render youth charming.

Dusk can be even more beautiful than dawn. The setting sun splashes ethereal colours and sketches myriad patterns across the evening sky. Nature seems most beautiful at twilight. So also, old age is sometimes more beautiful than childhood even because of the maturity one gains from the various lessons and experiences of life. One who has lived a true and full life does not fear old age. To one who has gained wisdom, old age is not frightening; it is a symbol of maturity and a time of knowledge.

After twilight comes night. At times, night is more beautiful than day. The world is awash with soft moonlight, and all is calm. We cannot find such tranquillity during the day. Similarly, death becomes a divine and blissful experience when one understands that it is not the end of life, only the beginning of another. Death becomes a divine experience for one who has transcended the physical and mental planes through spiritual practices such as meditation, worship and selfless actions. Such a person knows that death is just the next stage of life. Like a student waiting to enrol in university, one looks forward to death. Thus, even death becomes beautiful.

Spiritual knowledge is necessary if we want each moment of life to be beautiful and enjoyable. Those who have it will never fear death. Though the fear of death is the greatest of fears, death cannot touch one who has internalised spiritual principles and risen to the higher planes of God-consciousness. In reality, death happens every moment. We are born anew with every inhalation and die with every exhalation. Our body changes every moment. The body of our childhood is not the body of our youth. How we behave during childhood is also not how we behave in youth. The infant dies so that the child can be born, and the child dies so that the youth can be born. Only when the youth dies is the mature elder born. The word 'die' just means that the form and behaviour of the infant disappears as the infant grows into a child, for example. Thus, even though death happens at each stage, we consider only the death that takes place at old age. Death is nothing but a change, an evolution into the next stage of life.

Finally, Bhartruhari says,

Sarvam vastu bhayaanvitam bhuvi
Nrinaam vairagyameva abhayam.

Everything in this world causes fear. Vairagya is man's refuge from fear. Amma says love delivers one from fear. Amma is not talking about ordinary love but pure love for God. Where there is selfless love, there is no fear or grievance. When man becomes an embodiment of love, he gains the strength to overcome all fears. Therefore let us strive to become embodiments of love and immortality by performing our spiritual practices with enthusiasm and faith. This is the surest way to overcome fear.

17

The Universe – A Beautiful Symphony

This universe is the stage for a grand musical extravaganza. There is a wonderful orchestra playing here incessantly. But only hearts attuned to its music can relish it. This enchanting world—the trees, the sky, the birds, all other kinds of living beings, and the pulsations emanating from them all—is a vast and marvellous musical empire.

We are all part of *nada brahmam*, the primordial sound that subtly pervades the entire creation. God's music is pulsating in us incessantly. Life is a school that helps us manifest this music. We must learn how to tune ourselves to the cosmic music. Every instrument has its own sweetness, uniqueness and significance. Spirituality teaches us how to become one with the rhythm and tune of creation.

When the rhythm of life falters, we experience sorrow. When the rhythm of our *prana* (subtle life force) is upset, we fall sick. When the mind's rhythm goes awry, mental disease arises. When the rhythmic balance of the world is disturbed, natural calamities occur. In brief, creation is rhythmic in nature. Man alone violates this sacred rhythm. His actions are becoming artificial. Birdsong at dawn is never irksome. The chirruping of crickets at night never disturbs. The gruff croaking of frogs at the edges of ponds during the monsoon beautifully blends with the patter of rainfall. The sounds of nature are all melodious. It is the words and deeds emerging from man's selfishness that upset the natural rhythm in creation.

A king invited artists to paint pictures of the Himalayas. Several artists took part in the competition. They strove to capture on canvas the majestic beauty of the august mountains. The king appointed experts to choose the best painting but they could not. Every picture seemed better than the rest! They told the king that it was impossible to decide which one was the best. The king came to see the paintings for himself. He, too, realised that judging them was no easy task. Why, the paintings seemed to outdo the very Himalayas in beauty! The king asked each artist to explain their artwork. He thus appraised each and every work. When he came to the last painting, the artist unfurled the canvas featuring an exquisite depiction of the Himalayas. The artist slowly walked towards the picture, entered the frame, started scaling the mountains, and finally disappeared into the Himalayas! The king and the others present looked on in stunned silence as the artist disappeared into his art!

This is how the universe has been created. Though the whole creation is pervaded by God, He remains invisible. To know Him, we need to tune our mind to Him. For those who move in tandem with the cosmic rhythm, life becomes a divine experience.

Om purnamadah purnamidam purnat purnam udachyate
Purnasya purnam aadaaya purnam evaavasishyate

Om! That is fullness and this is fullness. From
the fullness, fullness is born. Remove the fullness
from the fullness and fullness alone remains.

This famous mantra from the *Brihadaranyaka Upanishad* clearly describes this divine experience.

God resides in all that is sentient and insentient. We usually say that God created the universe. It would be more accurate to say that God has become the universe. The creator abides in creation just as the artist resides invisibly in the artistic creation.

Only perfection can emerge from perfection. Even if we light thousands of lamps from a lamp, the light from the first lamp does not diminish. All the lamps will shine as bright as the first one.

Thus there are no imperfections anywhere. Let us pray to Amma for inner purity so that we can perceive perfection everywhere.

18

Eternal Bliss

Life is supposed to be a divine experience. It is we who make it beautiful or awkward. Whenever we become a part of creating beauty, everything becomes beautiful. Beauty is a creation; so, too, ugliness. Happiness is a creation; so, too, misery. All that we receive in this world is our own making. There is nothing we get that is not our own. Sowing what we reaped—that is the law of karma.

Life is like a blank wall. We can make it magnificent by painting pictures of beautiful scenery and many-coloured flowers. Or we can scrawl ghosts, apparitions and demons on it and thus create a horrible scene. God has left it to us. We can spin a beautiful dream or create a nightmare.

If we understand this, everything becomes easy. Making life beautiful is our responsibility. If being in the hell gives us happiness, we can choose it. If we cannot find joy there, we can leave it at once. We need not waste even a moment.

Life is a God-given opportunity. All that we need is here. From these raw materials, we can make whatever we want, how we want it. To do so, we need a Guru's help. The word 'Guru' is hard to translate into other languages. We lose several shades of meaning when it is translated as 'Master'. A Guru is not just a teacher but one who is capable of leading us to the Truth. Truth cannot be taught. It can only be acquired. The presence that enables us to achieve this is the Guru.

Amma once addressed a conference of scientists and technical experts in Mumbai. They asked Amma several questions, all of which She answered. When She asked them a question in turn, they fell silent. Amma asked, "What is more expansive than the outer space?" They had no answer.

Smiling, Amma said, "The inner world. What have you done to explore the mysteries of the inner world? Find the fountain of happiness within." Only those who have found the source of happiness within lead contented lives. For them, working is not different from worshipping the governing power that is the cause of the universe. All the skills they acquire are just instruments to tune into that supreme power. As far as such people are concerned, engaging in action is the same as worshipping God. When the sense of individuality disappears, all sorrows end.

"The Guru sits in silence. Even from that silence, the disciples assimilate all knowledge." This was the mode of instruction deemed ideal by the great rishis of ancient India.

Once an aspirant approached a Guru and said, "I went to several Gurus, but all of them failed me. None of them were true Gurus. I have come to You with great hope. You are my final refuge. Please protect me. I know You have the power to give me the ultimate knowledge. I can sense that special power radiating from You."

The Guru said, "Yes, I could do that. But so can the other Gurus you mentioned. I know them all. The question is not whether I bestow on you that knowledge but whether you have it in you to receive it."

The disciple said, "I am ready for anything. I'll do whatever You tell me."

The Guru said, "Then come with me. I'm going to fetch water from the well. Remember one thing: never ask any question. Questions are not allowed. Carefully observe and understand. You should not ask even a single question."

The disciple said, "That's not such a difficult thing to do." But from the outset, he started becoming restless. He saw the Guru fetching water with a bottomless bucket. The disciple wanted to blurt out, "What are you doing? Are you crazy?" But questions were not permitted. With great effort, he shut his mouth but for how long?

The Guru continued drawing water from the well using the bottomless bucket. As he drew the bucket up, the water would flow out. By the time the Guru brought the bucket out of the well, it would be empty!

The man began to have doubts about this Guru, too. He thought, "He is either crazy or a fool. What am I to get from this madcap? The other Gurus are better than this one."

As he was not supposed to ask questions, he kept quiet. But after the Guru had drawn out an empty bucket for the fourth time, the man blurted out, "What on earth are you doing? This is not how one should draw water from the well. This bucket has no bottom!"

The Guru said, "You broke the rule. You were not supposed to ask questions. You were told to observe and understand. Now, please leave. There is nothing I can do for you. You are just like that bottomless bucket. Even if I gave you everything, nothing would collect in you. You will lose it all. It will not benefit you or the world."

What the Guru expects from the disciple is total surrender and lifelong dedication. If we are ready to dedicate our life entirely, the Guru will take on all our karma and ultimately bestow Self-knowledge or God-realisation. For that, blind faith in the Guru is necessary. If we try to measure that unfathomable immensity with our intellect, we will end up agitated and thus fritter away this lifetime. There is a saying that it is easy to live with a sinner, but very difficult to live with a mahatma. For mahatmas constantly seek to uproot even the subtlest of vasanas from the disciples' minds.

All problems are creations of the mind. The mind is a troublemaker. But we can use the same mental energy to surmount problems, too. Spiritual practices are meant to tame the mind. The Guru teaches us how to tame the mind. The mind likes to do what seems pleasurable. Nevertheless, when we obey the mind's dictates, we lose our mental strength.

The Guru works against the whims of our mind. Therefore, the disciple might find His ways unpalatable. He might even try to find fault with the Guru's actions. But no matter what the disciple's thoughts and actions, the Guru's endless compassion and grace continue to flow towards him incessantly. When we acquire the purity of mind to receive it, complete surrender happens on its own.

19

The Female Voice on the Phone

Years ago a devotee of Amma in Kochi suffered from a heart disease. He was admitted to a nearby hospital where he soon recovered. Nevertheless, the doctor suggested that he undergo an expert examination at a hospital in Coimbatore, some hundred kilometres from Kochi

Accordingly, after he was discharged, he was taken to Coimbatore. The doctors there diagnosed three blocks in his coronary arteries and recommended surgery in a month.

His wife immediately brought him to Amritapuri. She told Amma all that the doctors had said. In tears, she prayed to Amma to help her husband avoid the surgery. Amma stroked his chest many times. Smiling reassuringly, She told him that there was nothing to be afraid of, and comforted the wife. She advised them to proceed with the doctor's suggestion. She assured them that She would be with them always. After returning home, his wife continued praying to Amma to save him without surgical intervention.

Finally, the day of the surgery arrived. The man was admitted to the hospital the previous day. All preparations for the surgery were made. The nurse administered a mild sedative, and shifted the husband to the operation theatre. At this time, the doctor received a phone call. A female voice repeatedly said, "This patient doesn't require a surgery." This was the first such experience he had had in his thirty years of medical service. The doctor was a pious man. He felt the message was God's warning to prevent something untoward from happening during the surgery. He postponed the surgery for the time being.

The doctor was well aware of the blocks that showed clearly in the angiogram. He decided to repeat the angiogram. Surprisingly, there were no blocks seen in the new angiogram! He kept the patient under observation for a few more days in the hospital and then discharged him, declaring him perfectly healthy.

To this day, the doctor does not know who called him on the phone and told him to cancel the surgery. As far as the patient and his relatives were concerned, it was Amma. When we realise that we are completely helpless, our ego dissolves, and Guru's grace flows towards us.

20

Divine Vision of Devi

A few years ago, a family came for Amma's darshan in Chennai, having seen programmes about Her annual Brahmasthanam Festival. They came to Amma with a complaint about their ten-year-old daughter.

All of a sudden, this little girl had lost her faith in God. She stopped praying and going to the temple. She refused to enter the puja room at home. She even started saying that her family was worshipping demonic forces instead of God.

Aghast at this sudden change in her, the parents asked her where she had gathered such ideas. She said, "Teacher said we should not worship demonic powers."

The parents had shifted their daughter to a convent school not long ago. The child believed the teacher more than her parents. When Amma heard their problem, She said, "Don't worry, Amma will take care of it."

After the Chennai programme ended, Amma returned to Amritapuri. A few days later, the parents and daughter came there to see Amma. There was a glow on the young girl's face that suggested that she had experienced something extraordinary. She seemed entirely transformed. She now wanted to be with Amma all the time.

Her parents related what had happened. One morning, they found the girl missing. She had been playing with friends in the courtyard earlier. They searched for her everywhere but could not find her. They informed the police, who found no trace of her. At last, that evening, someone spotted her in a temple nearby and brought her home. For some time, she was not able to speak.

The next day, she told her parents what had happened. She had been playing with friends when, looking up, she saw her teacher standing at the gate in front of her house. When the girl invited her inside, the teacher said that she was in a hurry, and wanted the girl to come with her. When the girl asked where they were going, the teacher said that she would tell her later. When she asked if she could first inform her parents, the teacher said, "No need! I shall inform them later."

The girl followed the teacher. They entered the precincts of a temple. The girl wondered why the teacher was going to the temple. Holding the girl by her hand, the teacher climbed the steps into the sanctum sanctorum, and disappeared inside! For a moment, the girl could not see anything. She only heard the conch blowing and temple bells ringing. Then the radiant form of Jagadamba (Mother of the Universe) became visible to her inside the sanctum sanctorum. She could not recall what happened after that.

When the temple priest arrived for the evening pujas, he saw the girl sitting in front of the shrine. When he asked her why she was sitting there alone, he did not receive any reply. The priest then informed her parents and took her home.

While the parents were telling Amma all this, She said smilingly, "As she had so much belief in her teacher's words, Devi had to take that form!"

That night, seeing Amma in Devi Bhava, the child whispered to her mother, "This is the exact form I saw in the temple!"

21

A Radiant Female Form at the Altar

Consecration ceremonies were being carried out in a temple near Ernakulam. I was invited there for the inauguration ceremony. The temple authorities had also invited a Christian devotee of Amma named Sebastian. In his talk, he related how he came to be associated with the temple.

Many years ago, his father, a government official in charge of public works, had demolished a temple in order to widen a road. The road could actually have been widened without demolishing the temple. This deeply hurt the devotees, some of whom salvaged the idol and preserved it reverentially. Taking it to the next village, they built a small temple for it.

Sebastian's father became paralysed and bedridden. He died soon after. His children also started getting afflicted by the same disease, and lost their lives, one by one. Sebastian, too, lay paralysed for months. Medical science was unable to diagnose or treat his ailment. He began to feel that his body, which he had considered most precious, was a burden. He had to depend on others for his every need. His only wish in life was to go to the bathroom on his own. He lost all hope in life. Even his close relatives and friends started ignoring him.

At that time, his friend, Joy Mathew, visited him one day. Joy spoke about Amma for a long time, and gave Sebastian Amma's biography. After reading the book, Sebastian began praying to Amma daily and derived immense strength. He also heard a voice within: "You will be healed soon."

The next day, someone from the local church came to invite Sebastian to a special prayer ceremony. They made necessary arrangements for him so that he could take part. Sebastian watched the priest as he interacted with the parishioners. Looking at the altar, he was wonderstruck to see another priest sitting there. On closer observation, he saw that it was no priest but a woman clad in white, an unusual scene, as ladies never enter the altar. She was wearing strings of rudraksha beads on her neck and wrists. A ray of light seemed to emanate from Her and enter his body. He felt a tremendous transformation happening within. He felt an unshakeable faith that he would soon be healed.

The very next day, he found that he could walk without anyone's help. In one week, he was fully healed. He telephoned Joy Mathew and told him about the miracle and expressed his desire to meet Amma as soon as possible.

The next Sunday, both of them went to see Amma. They arrived during bhajans. Seeing Amma's form, he was convinced that it was none other than Her who had appeared at the church altar. He became an ardent devotee of Amma and began spiritual practices in accordance with Her directions.

Wanting to share his experiences with others, he started giving spiritual discourses in many places. That is how he arrived in the old temple that his own father had demolished. Sebastian believed that speaking about it would atone for his father's sins.

Amma constantly reminds us about the value of meditation. Meditation is a life without words. It is the fullness of pure love, a love directed not towards any individual but all of creation. When we can love any circumstance, we are in the state of meditation. "I am the master. All these here are my slaves"—this is the belief of ego-consciousness. The devotee says, "All sentient and insentient beings are my masters, and I, their slave."

If we are dissatisfied, it only means that we have trained ourselves to be so. Dissatisfaction depends on the mental constitution. There are those who are discontented in any situation. Those minds have a remarkable ability to become unhappy about anything. If you spoke to them about the charm of a rose, they will start counting the thorns on the bush. If you say, "What a fine day!" they will stare at you in bewilderment and ask, "What's so special about it? It's just an interlude between two nights. Why express so much sentiment over it?"

Amma says that we ought not to waste time crying for worldly things; we ought to shed tears for God alone. Those tear drops can wash His feet and cleanse our own mind. If the mind is in our control, we can enjoy bliss even in the worst hell.

There is a scientific theory that postulates that the entire universe—with its millions of stars and thousands of galaxies and its unimaginable expansiveness—can be consolidated into a tiny space smaller than a hydrogen atom. This is the case with mahatmas like Amma. We can easily visualise a drop of water falling into the ocean. But here, we are talking about the ocean falling into a drop of water. That is the difference. A small human form accommodates the cosmic power in all its fullness. Amma makes this clear through the example of the tap and the tank. All the water in the tank is available through a small tap. Similarly, it is possible to experience the limitless power of God through the small body of a mahatma.

Pleasures are ephemeral whereas bliss is eternal. To wallow in fleeting pleasures is a waste of our life. Pleasures come and go. We must take a firm decision: I will strive for the eternal; I will strive to attain what even death cannot touch. Only one who has attained that can claim to have lived a true life.

The Guru alone can bless us with eternal bliss. We can experience that ultimate truth while still in this body. May Amma bless us all with that eternal bliss.

22

The Blessing of the Areca Tree

Can a tree bless? This question arose in my mind. Once, I even asked Amma this question. Many people may have this doubt. If trees did not bless, people would die for want of oxygen. For man to live peacefully in this world, he requires the blessings of everything sentient and insentient. In response to my query, Amma indeed showed me a tree that can bless!

The following incident took place in the ashram years ago. Amma was giving Devi Bhava darshan. A poor family came and told Amma about their problems. Their business had gone under, and they had lost everything. They had moved into a hut.

In those days, the crowds that came for darshan were not huge, and people could explain everything in detail to Amma. As I was sitting very close to Amma, I heard what this family said.

Amma told the father, "Son, bring an areca nut." I did not understand why. After darshan, they bought an areca nut from a nearby shop and came back. Amma infused Her breath into it and returned it to them, saying, "Plant it in front of your house, love it, and protect it. All your problems will be solved."

I was not very convinced. How could planting an areca nut solve man's problems? I thought that Amma was just consoling them. I forgot about this incident.

After a few years, when I went to a famous Devi temple, the family living next to the temple invited me to their home. I noticed an areca tree in their front courtyard. It had a small platform around it. "A platform around an areca?" I asked in surprise.

The man in that house replied, "We went to Amritapuri ashram years ago when we were facing many problems. Our business had failed. Though our daughter had already been married off, the marriage was on the rocks. At home, everyone was suffering from ailments. Seeing no solution in sight, we even contemplated suicide. It was then that a devotee brought us to Amma, who blessed an areca nut and gave it to us. All our problems were solved after that, such was the power of the areca nut Amma gave us!"

I asked, "What did you do with that areca nut?"

"We planted it in the front courtyard as Amma had advised. She had told us to love it. So from the next day onwards, we started loving and worshipping it. As advised, we watered it daily and added manure every day. As it grew, all our problems were being solved one by one. This mansion replaced our old hut."

I was still not convinced. I thought, if that was the case, would it not be enough to give everyone with problems an areca nut? Returning to Amritapuri, I asked Amma, "If areca nuts can solve problems, why not make them available at the book stall? Then Amma can get some rest instead of sitting here like this!"

Amma said, "There is a lot of value in many of the things we dismiss as worthless. Though there are complex problems in the world, their solutions are often simple." She said that the family had treated the areca nut as divine because Amma had given it to them. After planting it, they had observed with devotion as each leaf sprouted and grew big. Daily, they would water it with dedication, wave burning camphor before it reverentially, and garland it. Instead of seeing it as just a tree, they had venerated it as Devi Herself. If one tries to see the divine in a tree, God's blessings will flow towards us through the tree.

A jeweller can recognise a diamond whereas someone who does not know better might see it as just another stone. Likewise, the man who considers everything in this world useless, and his own life a curse, wastes his life. The great masters say that we ought to live in accordance with the *Purusharthas* (ordained objects of human pursuit), *viz. dharma* (cosmic law and order), *artha* (wealth), *kama* (desire) and *moksha* (liberation). Wealth may be earned through righteous means; there is nothing wrong with doing so. The money thus earned can be used to satisfy righteous desires. Finally, when we give all these up and separate the life force from the body, one will attain liberation, which brings eternal bliss. People are in a way doing all these things, but, in this Kali Yuga, kama has pride of place! We live to eat, and study to find a job and earn money.

Amma says that if even one person in a group of worldly people aspires for liberation, he will compensate for the others, just as the presence of one Amma compensates for millions of others! Through Her words and the faith devotees have in them, Amma is helping countless people in countless ways. Through a humble areca nut that costs not more than a penny, She solved problems that would probably not have been solved even through expensive ritual worship. In such instances, Amma says, "Love is of utmost importance. A life rooted in love and dharma ultimately ends all our sorrows."

23

Amma's Lucky Daughter

This story occurred in a place called Kodungalloor, the sacred land where Amma consecrated Her first Brahmasthanam temple.

On the first day of the Brahmasthanam temple festival, a devotee invited Amma to visit her home after darshan ended. Amma said, "Daughter, if time permits, Amma will come."

That day's darshan went on until daybreak the next day. Amma then went to the home of another devotee, who had for a long time been inviting Amma to visit her house. The devotee who had invited Amma the previous day was present in this house when Amma arrived.

On seeing her, Amma asked, "Daughter, is your home nearby?" She said that it would take at least forty-five minutes by car. Then Amma lovingly said, "This time, it will be difficult to travel so far. But when Amma comes here the next time or passes that way, please remind me, and Amma shall come."

Amma then asked this devotee to make Her a cup of tea. Overjoyed, she rushed to the kitchen and soon returned with some tea. Seeing her jubilation, Amma remarked, "See how happy she is! It's as if she has won the lottery!" Pointing at her, Amma merrily exclaimed, "Lottery! Lottery!" Some thought that Amma had given her a new name! The devotee was ecstatic at having been able to make tea for Amma. Her heart was full. It was as if Amma had visited her home.

Even after reaching home, she kept thinking about inviting Amma to her house. Then she began to have second thoughts about whether it would be appropriate. Her house was very small. If Amma and the ashram residents came, there would not even be standing space for them.

Suddenly, she recalled Amma's words: "Lottery! Lottery!" What did Amma mean, she wondered? She felt that Amma might have been hinting to her to buy lottery tickets in order to help tide over her financial difficulties. As Amma had uttered the word 'lottery' twice, she decided to buy two lottery tickets. She did and both won prizes! With that money, she built a good house.

Later, when I visited that area, she invited me home, requesting that I perform the house warming ceremony. I accepted the invitation, went to her beautiful house, and conducted the ceremony.

This story is reminiscent of the story of Kuchela from the life of Lord Krishna. Kuchela was a close childhood friend and devotee of the Lord. When he came to Dwaraka for the first time to meet the Lord, he had only a little flattened rice as an offering. The Lord grabbed it and enjoyed two handfuls of it with great relish. Within minutes, Kuchela became the richest man in the world. Kuchela received not just material prosperity; he was also uplifted to spiritual heights. Similarly, this devotee had become deserving of Amma's limitless grace by her innocent love, devotion and faith.

The story does not end here. Many years later, in a discourse I gave at Kodungalloor during the Brahmasthanam festival, I recounted this incident. The woman who had won the lottery was present. She was doing service in the kitchen. She told the others, "All of you, please listen. Swamiji is talking about me!"

Hearing the story, a devotee from Ernakulam, who was also engaged in service in the kitchen, approached her and said, "Please get me a lottery ticket as well!"

After Amma's programme, she bought him a lottery ticket from a nearby shop. He won a prize! During Amma's Ernakulam Brahmasthanam festival, She also visited his home.

How can such miraculous events be explained? One can only attribute them to the Guru's grace. What makes one eligible for that shower of grace is unalloyed faith. Indeed, childlike innocence is most important.

Reading this story, we need not try to force a cup of tea on Amma! The sweetness of our love is enough to obtain Her grace. Innocent faith arises from immense love for the Guru. May Amma bless us to live with such childlike innocence and purity, and thereby overcome all sorrows of life to attain eternal bliss.

24

Christian Teacher and Krishna Picture

We see so many faces in the journey of life. We might not remember all of them, and may well forget even significant events. But there are some incidents we can never forget. One such experience happened during my school days.

Saramma Teacher taught us mathematics in the fifth grade. One day, Teacher gave us a few questions and asked us to answer them in the class itself. I finished solving all the problems very quickly. I used to draw pictures of Lord Krishna during my leisure. As I had finished solving the problems, I took a piece of paper and started drawing. I did not notice Teacher coming and standing behind me to watch what I was doing. Before I could complete the picture, Teacher came round and stood in front of me. All the children were afraid of Teacher, who was short-tempered. Raising her voice, She said, "Stand up!" There was pin-drop silence. "Drawing pictures when I told you to work on the problems?" Teacher's eyes became red with anger. The other children sat with bated breath. All eyes were on me. I did not know what to say. I stood there like an offender, head hung low. "Where are the sums I gave you?" She examined my book. She saw that I had answered all the questions correctly. She then took the picture I had drawn and stared at it for a long time. Stepping closer to me, she softly asked, "Can I have this?" I nodded my head in assent. A smile lit up her face. All the children heaved a sigh of relief. Teacher slowly walked away and sat on her chair.

Years later, one day, I received a phone call from AIMS Hospital, Kochi. The caller informed me that Saramma Teacher, who had taught me in school, was coming to the Ernakulam Ashram. We met that evening. When she entered the ashram office, I stood up. She had changed. The changes were those wrought by time. I observed her aged face. The old liveliness and toughness were gone. She stood silently, gazing at my face for a long time. In those moments, neither of us said anything. A little later, in hushed voice, she asked me, "You've become a great person, haven't you? Do you remember me?" Her eyes were brimming with tears. Unable to reply, I, too, remained silent. "In case you forgot, I brought a token of recognition." She hurriedly took out a folded sheet from her bag and passed it to me. Opening it, I saw the picture of Sri Krishna I had drawn years ago! I was surprised that she had preserved it for more than forty years! My eyes, too, became moist. Teacher did not want to sit down. I had to force her.

Teacher then explained the circumstances leading to our meeting after all these years. "Swamiji, I see you on TV. For a long time, I've wanted to meet you in person. I knew you were in Amma's ashram. Though I had heard a lot about Amma, it is only recently that I had the good fortune of meeting Her. I hadn't told anybody there that I was Swamiji's teacher. However, as soon as Amma saw me, She called out to others, 'Here is Sreemon's teacher!' I started crying."

After darshan, she looked for me. That was when she learnt that I was in the Ernakulam ashram. "Today, when I came to AIMS Hospital, I decided that I would leave only after meeting you."

The experiences we have in life are not meaningless. There are definite reasons behind them.

When she was about to leave, she said, "Please return the picture to me." When I passed it to her, she pressed it to her heart and said, "I'll preserve it until my death. It is on account of this picture of Sri Krishna that I came to have the good fortune of receiving Mata Amritanandamayi's blessings. I have nothing more to achieve in life. My life has been fulfilled."

Before she bid me goodbye, she entrusted me with a note to be offered to Amma. She had written,

To Amma, the Great Master,

I am aware that Christ and Krishna are in Amma. When I met You, the truth that God is Love became obvious to me. Please be kind enough to have a space for this humble self, too, in Your loving heart.

With kisses on Your feet,

Sreemon's teacher.

25

An Invocation to Wisdom

Before meeting Amma, I imagined that technology could solve all of man's problems. But as technology advanced, man's problems became more aggravated. He does not seem to have become happier.

In those days, I used to imagine that all scientists were atheists. When I joined the Raman Research Institute after my studies, I saw that there were believers among scientists. The sight of scientists forgetting hearth and home and spending long hours in their laboratories with an attitude of self-sacrifice, amazed me.

Among the top scientists there was a Christian woman, who was also my boss. She gave me a piece of advice: "You're going to do research on solar radiation. Please chant the Gayatri Mantra a few times before you start, because it is impossible to become successful in both research and life without intuition."

When we have to make sudden decisions in life, intellectual knowledge alone will not help. One wrong decision is enough to wipe out our achievements and destroy our life. We must feel the right answers from within. That can happen only if one has a certain degree of inner purification. Chanting the Gayatri Mantra can give us that purity:

Om bhur bhuvah svah
Tat savitur varenyam
Bhargodevasya dheemahi
Dhiyo yo nah prachodayat

We meditate on the effulgent glory of the divine light.
May He inspire our intelligence.

The Gayatri Mantra is a prayer that arose spontaneously from the heart of the rishi who perceived the Sun God. As he stood gazing at the rising sun, he prayed, "O Sun God, You illumine all the worlds. You are worthy of worship. I rely on You. Please illumine and inspire my intellect, too!" It was a prayer for the dawning of inner knowledge.

The Sun God illumines the sun of this world and the suns of all the worlds. The millions of galaxies in the infinite Universe are all suns. The prayer was directed at the Sun within, the inmost Self, which illumines the suns of even worlds we do not know.

The rishis were seers of mantras. They knew the secrets of mantras. Theirs was not knowledge based on hearsay but direct experience. The rishis experienced the infinite power that illumines the cosmos, and proclaimed this truth for the benefit of the entire world. The rishis did not compose the mantras; they perceived them. Each mantra has a presiding deity. If chanted while contemplating the form of that deity, the mantra will yield more results. Incessant chanting is required to gain the results of chanting a mantra.

Water boils at a temperature of 100 degrees Celsius. If further heated, it becomes steam, which is more powerful than water. The steam engine gives us an idea of how powerful steam is. Similarly, every time the mantra is chanted, it acquires greater potency. It is said that a mantra must be repeated millions of times to actualise its potency.

In the Satya Yuga, the Age of Truth, the environment was spiritually pure. The age could also be described as the mantra yuga. Now *yantras* (machines) have replaced mantras. Yantras now do what mantras did. A time will come when even yantras won't suffice. The future will see the age of cunning machinations. In ancient times, strength was demonstrated on the platform of warfare. In future, victory will not be determined on the basis of strength but cunning. The divine seers saw that the only way to remain untouched by sorrow, whatever the yuga, is to rise to the realm of God. Out of compassion, they shared their knowledge with us.

Every mantra begins with *Om*, also known as the Pranava mantra because it pulsates in all creation. Through 'Om,' the rishi says all there is to say. Om alludes to the four states: the wakeful, dream, deep sleep and *turiya* (meaning 'the fourth') states. The first three stages are represented by *bhur-bhuva-svah*, i.e. the three worlds: *bhu loka, bhuvar loka* and *svar loka*. The first is earth, i.e. the familiar gross world. This is not the only world that exists. There are higher and lower worlds. Of the higher worlds, man has access to are *bhu loka, bhuvar loka* and *svar loka*. To go beyond them, one needs to have acquired more *punya* (spiritual merit). The four worlds beyond are *mahar loka, jana loka, tapo loka* and *satya loka*. Then there are other *upa lokas* (subsidiary worlds) like *indra loka, chandra loka, surya loka* and *pitru loka*. The nether worlds are also seven: *atala, vitala, sutala, talatala, rasatala, mahatala* and the lowest of all, *patala. Jnanis* (the Self-realised) can create heaven anywhere. Mahatmas cannot be put in hell. For, even if they are, they will make a heaven of hell!

Those who have awakened into the world of divine experience perceive heavenly beauty everywhere. They create heaven everywhere. The Gayatri Mantra raises us to this realm of intuitive experience.

When chanted by an enlightened Guru, all mantras are equally powerful. When Amma initiates us into a mantra, She is not saying but instilling in us the power of the mantra, which becomes embedded in us, like a seed. On chanting it repeatedly, it grows into a mighty tree. The more we chant, the more powerful it becomes. Subsequently, the mantra-tree yields fruit. Once we obtain the fruit of the mantra, the course of our life changes. The route to God becomes much easier. Then every word we utter becomes a mantra.

Someone wanted to pray to God but did not know how. In deep anguish, he wrote down whatever letters he knew and prayed: "O, God, I don't know any prayer. Please create a fine prayer from these letters and accept it!"

He then heard a voice: "Child, yours is the heartiest prayer I have ever heard!"

Hearing this, the pious man's eyes filled with tears. Among prayers, God likes most the prayer of one who does not know how to pray. Whatever we utter is a mantra. So, we must not speak carelessly for our words may come true! The vibrations of anything we utter will linger in nature and come back to us. So we must be careful while speaking. The tongue plays a key role in managing the sorrows of life. Therefore, if we tame the tongue, we can succeed in life easily. The tongue has two functions: talking and tasting. It likes to talk and relish tasty food. It is one sense with two functions. If we can control the tongue, we can control all the senses. The tongue alone is enough to cause one's downfall. If used correctly, one can transcend all sorrow and rise up to the divine. The rishis advised us on how to use the tongue properly. May all that is uttered become a prayer. This happens when whatever we say is done with love. May all our words be echoes of love.

Beholding the rising sun, the rishi prayed. He did not see the sun as a mere fireball. He imagined it as the Sun God, who imparts brilliance, energy and strength to the whole world. If the sun didn't rise, if there were no sunrays, there would be no life in the world. On seeing the sun that gives strength and energy to the whole world, the rishi did not find it difficult at all to conceive it as the manifestation of God. That is why he prayed, "O Sun God. You illumine all the three worlds. You are worthy of worship."

The Gayatri Mantra has three parts: extolling God, contemplating God, and praying to Him. Beholding the rising sun, the rishi said, "O Sun God, who illumines all the three worlds." He was not referring to just the sun that we see. The Sun God sheds light on all the three worlds. Who is He? This was praying to the divine effulgence that illumines the sun, moon, fire and all. The Sun God reflects the power of the Self. It is divine energy that manifests as the light of fire. "O Sun God, You illumine the three worlds. You are worthy of worship. I meditate on that divine light. May you lead my intellect in the right direction. May my intellect be inspired by Your light."

Intuitive knowledge can never be untrue. If words are to emerge from intuition, the ego must disappear. Ignorance must vanish. This darkness can be dispelled only when the Sun of Knowledge dawns.

26

Nine Holy Nights

Mahatmas have transcended birth and death. They do not feel that they have a body. To an astronaut, there is no sunrise and sunset. If there is sunrise, there is sunset; if there is sunset, there is again a sunrise. However, to a space traveller, these are just imaginings or sleights of hand that nature conjures. Similarly, in our perspective, a body has birth and death. But if we rise to extrasensory planes, we will find neither birth nor death. The moment we realise that we are not restricted to the body, we will have attained liberation from birth and death. People of such a realization are known as jnanis. Life is an opportunity to acquire this knowledge. But first, the nights of ignorance must vanish and the golden dawn of knowledge must arrive. The Goddess of Knowledge must shine within. The Navaratri celebrations (nine-day-long worship of Devi) aim at this.

The first three days are dedicated to the worship of Goddess Durga, the next three to Goddess Lakshmi, and the last three to Goddess Saraswati. This does not mean that there are many gods; no, there is only one God. The rishis called Him *brahma chaitanyam* (infinite effulgence). Being omnipotent, God can assume any form or remain formless. The gods or deities we worship are crystallizations of one or more of the infinite attributes of the one God. It is difficult to conceive of all the attributes together. Therefore we worship select attributes. Worship any one attribute, and all the others will follow.

Divine power is an enigmatic phenomenon. Some find beauty most endearing; the maternal (or paternal) form appeals to some others. For yet others, what draws them might be the idea of the Divine as remover of obstacles, goddess of knowledge or almighty power, for example. The formless God thus assumes forms, which we worship as deities.

Amma gives the following example: a woman is a teacher at school, mother to her child, daughter to her father, wife to her husband, and sister to her brother. These are the different roles played by one person, and not five people. Likewise, the rishis creatively depicted God's infinite attributes as deities, and gave us the freedom to worship any form we like. These sages even revealed ways of knowing God suited to an atheist! Amma says that whether someone believes in God or not is not important. If an atheist serves and loves the world selflessly, God will be ever ready to serve him.

During Navaratri, Durga, the Goddess of Warfare, is worshipped for the first three days. One may wonder why She holds so many weapons in Her many hands. The surgeon requires different kinds of instruments, which trained assistants pass him. However, Devi does not need any assistant as She has several hands of her own! These hands wield invisible weapons that can annihilate our ego and mental impurities. The sword in Kali's hand is no ordinary sword, but the sword of love and knowledge. The crowns of the ego bow down to love alone. No one hesitates to bow down to Amma, for heads involuntarily bow down in reverence to maternal love.

By worshipping Durga, we are really invoking Amma's Guru aspect. Our enemies are not outside; they are within. Without rooting out these enemies, i.e. our negativities, we cannot enjoy peace in life. Therefore, we must first annihilate our own demoniac aspects with the help of Durga. When the negativities disappear, all prosperity is ours. That is why we worship Goddess Lakshmi, the Goddess of Prosperity, over the next three days. Once enriched by true wealth, i.e. noble qualities that replace the negativities, Saraswati, the Goddess of Knowledge appears. There are no weapons in Her hands, only the melodious *veena* (a musical instrument). The dawn of inner knowledge makes life as sweet as a beautiful melody. Only knowledge can dispel the darkness of sorrow. Unless we surrender our ego, the Goddess within will not awaken. With the awakening of the Goddess of Knowledge, the nine-day-long worship comes to an end, and the tenth day is celebrated as the day of success. Therefore, to succeed in life, we must awaken the Goddess of Knowledge within.

If we can become as charming as an innocent child, Mother Nature will reveal to us Her treasure trove of mysteries. While the so-called civilised societies of today were still living in dense forests, the ancient sages of India had already composed entire volumes on celestial bodies and cosmic phenomena. Several branches of knowledge dawned within them, who lived in total harmony with nature, without the help of any gadget. All knowledge dawns within when the heart becomes pure. During Navaratri, we are engaged in purifying observances. Its concluding phase is worship of Saraswati. That done, we dedicate all the knowledge gained to God, and then start learning the alphabets. We become like a child, who has the attitude of a beginner. That is the aim of Navaratri.

All the knowledge that Kalidasa gained, which even scholars of repute cannot dream about, were the blessings of the Divine Mother of the Universe. He earned these blessings through his *dasa bhava*, or servant-like attitude of surrender. Knowledge obtained from such an attitude alone is real knowledge. Navaratri helps us to cultivate this attitude of surrender.

Kalidasa was taken to be a dullard or fool. He was seen chopping the very branch on which he was seated. Are we not also doing the same thing? We are all seated atop the branches of desire. It is just a matter of time before we fall. Some of us are chopping at the tree of longevity, comprising our own lives.

Seeing Kalidasa chopping the branch, some scholars contrived to get the fool married to a woman who had defeated them in debate, to settle scores with her. She only discovered that her husband was a dunce after marriage. However, she was still not ready to admit defeat. She resolved to make her stupid husband a genius. She sent him to a Kali temple for prolonged worship. Reaching the temple, he entered straight into its sanctum sanctorum and shut the door behind him! A little while later, someone knocked on the door. He did not open the door but remained seated. It was Mother Kali! She called out, "Who's inside?" He did not want to reply before finding out who was outside. He asked, "Who outside?"

Kali said, "It's Kali!"

At that, he said, "It's your dasa (servant) inside!" Thus he became Kali's dasa or Kalidasa. Devi cannot help blessing one who has the dasa attitude. Her compassion poured forth in a torrent. With her spear, she inscribed mantras on his tongue, thus showering Her grace on his egoless self. She opened the storehouse of all knowledge to him. Thus, one who had been regarded as a fool started singing lofty verses incessantly. He sang hymns seeing Devi right before his eyes. He went on to become the greatest bard the world ever saw, a mahatma. When there is a dasa attitude, God can invoke all knowledge in no more than an instant.

We all have the feeling of 'I' and 'mine.' Everyone says 'I'. What is the difference between two 'I's? Amma says, "You are the 'I' in me and I am the 'you' in you." There is no difference between both. The only difference is that our 'I' is confined to the body whereas Amma's 'I' pervades all of creation. There is only one 'I.' Only bodies appear different. To one who knows that the entire universe is connected to oneself, there is no other. Amma inhabits the world where there are no others. As there are no others, there is no feeling of separation or difference either, only the feeling of oneness.

There is no rest for a mahatma like Amma, who can converse with several worlds at the same time. However, She says that, for Her, abiding in the state of not doing anything while doing everything is rest. Many of us are all too eager to publicise the things we do: "Who drew this?" "I." "Whose is this?" "Mine." "Who made this?" "I." For us, the answer to everything is 'I'. Not so for Kalidasa. Because he thought of himself as a servant, he received God's grace in abundance. The mysteries of the universe were unveiled to him. Only one who has the dasa bhava can attain Self-knowledge. Amma's love is capable of creating the dasa attitude. We become nothing before this ocean of love. Amma instructs not through words but deeds. Even Her critics become like children in Her presence, forgetting everything else.

In America, a group of sceptics from a TV channel grilled Amma with a volley of questions. She spent hours speaking to them. They asked highly critical questions. By the end of the interview, the last questioner stood waiting for Amma's darshan. Everyone was surprised to see him lie in Amma's lap and cry. The cameraman and the rest of the crew followed suit. When their darshan ended, they stood there. Someone asked them, "Aren't you guys leaving?"

They said, "We need to but can't!"

Even though it is not possible to define God, we usually refer to him as *sat-chit-ananda* (truth-consciousness-bliss). Sat means ultimate reality. Chit is pure consciousness. Ananda is not the pleasure or happiness that we enjoy but an inexplicable intuitive experience. Though these three terms manifest the various aspects of God, He is beyond all these definitions. He is an indefinable intuitive experience. By truth, we mean what remains unchanged in this world of flux. Those who have not known the changeless substratum will not be able to enjoy life. To experience true joy, the sages said that we must know the ultimate truth.

There is a humorous story about God's creation. Having created a beautiful world, He created man (it seems man was created before woman). Having created man, God was satisfied and retired to His room to rest. Someone knocked on the door. Opening the door, He saw man standing there. He said, "God, I am all alone in this beautiful world. I need company."

God tried His best to dissuade him: "Will you get bored if you constantly enjoyed the beauty of nature?" But it did not work. God then went to His workshop, but He had used up all the raw materials. How to create something anew? Finally, summoning all the birds and beasts, God announced that He was withdrawing certain things from them. He created something new from what he withdrew: a charming damsel! God felt proud of His own creation, which He gifted man. Man did not imagine that God could create something so beautiful. He took woman with him. God again retired to His room, hoping to rest for a few days.

A little while later, there was a knock on the door again! It was man again: "I wanted company but now I've lost all my peace of mind on account of woman. Sometimes, she is full of love. At other times, she's like a nightingale, and at yet other times, like a vampire." (The reason was that she had been created from different living beings.) "Please take her back. I prefer to remain alone."

God took woman back and again retired to His room. Shortly, there was a knock on the door. It was man again. "What now?" God asked.

"Though she's irritating, I can't do without her!"

God returned woman to him. Confident that there would not be no problem again, He went back to rest. Hearing the man calling once again, God opened the door. "I can't live with her. I can't live without her!"

This time, God became angry. Glaring at man, He said, "I don't ever want to see you here again. Handle this problem yourself!"

It is man who creates misery in this charming world. We do not know that God is immanent in creation, and that is why the world appears miserable. God alone exists incognito, not the diverse forms. Change affects only names and forms. Truth refers to the changeless. One who knows that that the changeless is the substratum of the whole universe enjoys bliss. In olden times, the human lifespan was a hundred years. The first twenty five were the *brahmachari* phase or the student life. It was a time for gaining the strength to face life, a period for gaining mental control. This was followed by the *grihastha ashrama*, the house-holder phase. The *vanaprastha ashrama* or retirement followed. The final phase was *sanyasa ashrama*, the renunciate phase. It is also possible to proceed straight to sanyasa from brahmacharya.

A day will come in our life when we categorically declare that we do not want anything. Then and there, we can embrace sanyasa. It is because of our rigid ego that we suffer. Sorrow cannot touch one who lives in harmony with nature. Some, having understood the mysteries of nature, go straight to sanyasa, seeking only God. Some, who are yet to gain sufficient maturity from life experiences, will arrive there only after passing through the other stages (*ashramas*). No ashrama is above any other. Ultimately, all are destined to become *sanyasis*. The gods are eagerly waiting to bear witness to that scene. Miseries remind the godless of God.

In the olden days, marriage was also like sanyasa. A sanyasi takes an oath before the fire god that he will sacrifice his life for the well-being of all creation. The implication of marriage was very similar. One who has lived a self-centred life until then sheds his selfishness and sacrifices his life for another person's happiness. Upon the birth of a child, father and mother are ready to sacrifice their comforts for the sake of the child. In due course, the whole family vows to sacrifice their comforts for the sake of the world. Nowadays, because people enter into relationships only to gratify selfish desires, relationships crumble easily.

Amma says that every man and woman is *ardhana-reeswara*—a God who is half-man, half-woman. To evoke the feminine qualities in a man, the help of a woman is necessary. Similarly, to evoke the masculine qualities in a woman, the help of a man is necessary. Once these complementary qualities are awakened, they can transcend the qualities altogether. The couple can develop a bond of mutual reverence, beholding and worshipping the divine in each other. In vanaprastha (literally, taking to the forest), one need not leave one's residence to travel to a forest. Entrusting one's children with one's bank account, keys, etc. and focussing one's attention on spiritual matters is vanaprastha. Sanyasa is total detachment. It means going beyond the plane of service while living in the world with the awareness that one has completely dedicated oneself to God. When the body becomes an instrument that manifests all the attributes of God, others will rejoice in our presence. Even birds and beasts will forget their enmity in front of us.

In the olden days, people chanted the Gayatri Mantra in order to acquire strength. Our sages began chanting it while gazing at the rising sun. Doing so, they strove to awaken the sun of knowledge within. In the outer sun, they perceived that sun which was their own inner self, which illumines all celestial bodies. Amma says that there is a lamp glowing in each of us, one that can never be extinguished. Darkness can never touch him who knows that divine radiance shining within. Love gushes forth from one who is a true spiritual being. A spiritual person is not interested in attracting anyone's attention for he has shed his ego consciousness entirely. Such a person is no longer an individual. Where individuality disappears, God manifests wholly.

Amma says that worldly love is full of expectation. "If you love me, I will love you. If you provide me with all that I need, I shall love you." Such is the world. People will be ready to love us for money or if, and only if, they are given what they want. In contrast, the love of mahatmas is of a different order. Their love is unconditional. It is beyond differences of caste, creed, colour and religion. There will be many to share our fortunes but none to share our sorrows. Mahatmas like Amma demand only our bundle of woes. In return, She showers on us unconditional love.

27

Mysteries of Meditation

Almost everyone wants to know others' secrets. However, we remain ignorant of our own inner secrets. To know them, we need to understand the mysteries of *dhyana* (meditation) and do spiritual practises. Dhyana is the state of doing nothing. Usually, we are engaged in incessant physical or mental activity. We keep doing from the beginning of life until the end. We do not consider what might happen when all these works stop. Meditation is a journey along life's unknown terrains. We live in a world that is knowable only through the senses. The information supplied by the five senses is not always true. Our ears cannot hear all kinds of sounds. Our eyes cannot see all kinds of rays. Our nose cannot detect all scents. Nevertheless, we live in this world, taking the knowledge supplied by the senses to be correct. Most of us do not strive to attain the most precious knowledge. When all activity ceases, we rise to a plane of experience we have never had so far—the extrasensory plane of divine experiences! There are many levels of experience beyond the body, mind and intellect. To access these planes of intuitive experience, we need to be trained in meditation.

We reach the state of meditation when all physical, mental and intellectual activities come to a standstill. While we may have knowledge of many things in the outer world, we know next to nothing about the inner world because we have never striven to know what is happening within.

The *Bhagavad Gita* begins:

Dharma kshetre Kurukshetre
Samaveta Yuyutsavah
Mamakah Pandavaschaiva
Kimakurvata Sanjayah?

Dhritarashtra, the blind emperor, asks Sanjaya what is going on in the Kurukshetra battlefield. The king was blind by birth. His queen courted blindness willingly. No wonder their offspring were unrighteous! The king was blinded by parental love and attachment. The mother who assumed blindness was never in a position to oversee and control her children. We are all emperors of the empire of our inner world. We have never tried to understand the tumult of the inner world. We begin that enquiry for the first time only when we start practising meditation. Dhritarashtra's query about what is going on in Kuruskhetra—which is also called dharmakshetra, the field of dharma—marks the beginning of meditation. While we sit to meditate, we listen to what is happening in one's inner world. That is when we understand that there an incessant war going on. It is a war between our positive and negative tendencies, and conducive and adverse elements of our personality. Training is necessary to curb the entire Kaurava army. Meditation practices give us this training.

In our inner *Mahabharata War*, we must annihilate the six foes—attachment, wrath, greed, delusion, egotism and envy—and awaken the divine aspects within. This begins at the physical level. Initially, we must gain the ability to keep still for a prolonged period of time. We need not worry about concentration then. The two essentials for meditation practice are 1. the ability to sit unmoving in the same posture for a protracted period of time; and 2. the fruition of the mantra. We can achieve anything if we desperately need it. In Africa, there is a species of venomous snakes that can see only moving objects. If we were made to sit amidst them, we would acquire the ability to sit still for any amount of time! We thus have capabilities that awaken only when desperately needed.

Story of the Milkmaid

There is a famous story of an ordinary homemaker. During Emperor Shivaji's reign, the woman who used to deliver milk to the palace arrived late one day. By the time she delivered the milk and was leaving, the doors of the fort had closed. She begged the guards to open the doors, but they refused saying, "The doors will be opened only the next morning. King's orders!" All her entreaties fell on deaf ears. She was desperate to leave as she had left her young child home alone. She roamed around the palace premises frantically. Darkness fell. At some corner, she climbed over the fort wall and made her way home, where she found her child crying in hunger.

The next day, the king learned about what had happened. He found it hard to believe that an ordinary woman could scale the massive ramparts protecting them from enemies. The soldiers took her around the wall, for they wanted to know where the breach was. When she came to the spot from which she had escaped, she almost fainted when she noticed the sheer height of the cliff on which the fort was built! How in the world had she made her way down? By the power of maternal love. Similarly, we can gain the strength to perform many feats that seem impossible.

Mantra chanting helps control thoughts. The mind is a flow of thoughts. One thought does not make a mind just as a drop of water is not a river; millions of water drops make a river. Similarly, a mind is the coming together of many thoughts. Pictures in motion create a movie. Likewise, the universe is a reflection of the mind-flow. If a river flowed in many directions, its current will not be strong. If we can divert the tributaries along a single channel, the flow will be so powerful that we can generate electricity from it using turbines. In the same way, if we can gather the scattered rays of the mind, we can tap into its enormous potential.

If we ask Amma something, She usually says, "Amma will make a *sankalpa* (resolve)." As the currents of mahatmas' minds are immensely powerful, whatever they resolve becomes true. In contrast, the thought streams of our mind are flowing in innumerable directions. One who practices meditation tries to make these diverse streams flow in one direction. If we succeed in doing so, the treasure trove of wonders will open up to us.

A man visited his friend, who had been watching only one channel on his TV. "Why watch the same boring programmes everyday?" He installed many more channels on the TV so that his friend became spoilt for choice! We are like the friend, taking what we see to be reality and our successes to be real. When we realise that there are many other realms of intuitive experience and that we can enjoy even more beautiful divine experiences, we will be ready to seek the Self. We will start disciplining the mind by reining in our desires. All fortunes will rush to serve such a person.

This is the concept behind the image of Lord Vishnu reclining on Ananta, the many-headed serpent. He is in yogic sleep. Would we dare to sleep in a room in which there is just one snake? A tiny snake can kill our sleep! Here, the snake symbolises desire. So, a single keen desire can disturb our sleep. Each one of us is a carrier of multiple desires. One who has turned inward and directed his thousand desires to God becomes worthy of Vishnuhood. Such a person will be attended to by Lakshmi, Goddess of Prosperity. This is represented by the image of Lakshmi Devi seated at Vishnu's feet. The Lord resides on an ocean of milk. The white of milk symbolizes purity. When our mind becomes as pure as milk, all prosperity will come in search of us. The Lord's yogic sleep is no ordinary sleep. He is aware of the pulsations of all sentient and insentient beings in creation within himself. His sleep is not unconsciousness but the ultimate consciousness. There is not much difference between *bodha* (awareness), dhyana and samadhi. Sleep is meditation in unconsciousness. Meditation is sleep in consciousness. Dhyana can be likened to sleep, except that in sleep, we are unconscious.

Most people are familiar with the three states: the wakeful state, dream state, and the deep sleep state. There is a fourth state known as turiya. Only one who has awakened to this state knows the secrets of creation. Only one who knows these backstage secrets can enjoy the play of life. Otherwise, life will be like a battlefield. Mahatmas know that the world is a playground and not a battlefield. They know that the din and tumult of the world are not real. There might be dreadful scenes in a magic show but the magician knows that there is nothing to fear. Like this, although the miseries of life may appear real at the levels of the body, mind and intellect, they are unreal in the realm of the self. Even death can become a joyous divine experience.

Meditation is instructive. It enables us to relish the sweetness of death while still in the body. Death is not a state of non-being but the momentous point at which we are freed from the prison house of the body. The *Upanishads* proclaim, "O man, learn the technique of separating yourself from your body even before it decays!" That is meditation, which brings about the death of the ego and body consciousness, and the end of sorrow. Through meditation, we can transcend all the limitations that affect body and mind, and soar into the bliss of immortality. Death is not the end of life. It could be called a promotion. The sages who succeeded in enjoying the sweetness of death while still alive described it as the bliss of samadhi, the divine experience that rises when desires set. To enjoy that bliss, we must transcend time. When the mind disappears, time disappears as well. Time exists on the basis of the mind. It shrinks in moments of happiness and expands in times of sorrow. Time moves fast in heaven and ploddingly slowly in hell! The only way to transcend time is to stop the mind. The mind being a flow of thoughts, how can we stop the mind?

The Mind Genie

Once, a poor farmer approached a saint and asked for a mantra that would make him rich. The saint said, "I don't know any such mantra." Undaunted, the farmer kept pestering him. Finally, the saint said, "I shall give you a mantra. If you chant it, a genie will appear before you. He will grant you any boon you ask for. But remember one thing: go on asking. Keep him engaged in some work. Once he has not work left, he will devour you!"

The farmer said, "That's no problem. I've thousands of desires! I'll keep him engaged with all that."

He ran to his hut and chanted the mantra. The genie appeared and asked. "What does my master want?"

The farmer said, "I want to become the richest man in the world."

It was done in a moment. "Next?"

"A golden palace and some ten thousand attendants." The very next moment, a golden palace materialized. Ten thousand attendants stood ready.

"Now what?" the genie asked.

The farmer said he wanted his wife to become the most beautiful woman in the world. At once, his wife was transformed into a stunning beauty.

"Next?"

"Make me handsome!" Done.

Thus, the farmer went on listing his desires, one after another. Each one was fulfilled instantly. Finally, he had nothing left to ask. Not knowing what more to ask, he stood confounded. The genie advanced towards him, ready to devour him. Terrified, the farmer ran to the saint and threw himself at his feet. The saint said, "Tell the genie to make a sky-high flag mast. After he has erected it, order him to climb up and down the pole indefinitely until he is told to stop."

The technique worked. The genie was confined to the pillar.

The genie is our mind, which can help us satisfy any desire. The mind is capable of solving all problems. It can also be our undoing. If we do not know how to control the mind-genie, life can become miserable. When the disciple meets the Master, the first thing he ought to ask for is how to control this genie. The Guru initiates the disciple into a mantra, which is the sky-high mast that will arrest the genie. Like the genie who constantly asks, "What next?" the mind keeps chattering. Mantra chanting helps us arrest the mind.

Meditation and the Churning of the Milk Ocean

The story from the *Bhagavata* of the churning of the milk ocean signifies the various stages in meditation. The first thing to surface during the churning was the deadly poison called *kalakoodam*. As it was lethal enough to destroy the whole world, Lord Parameswara drank it. Similarly, during meditation, the impure thoughts of our mind will arise. We must offer them to the Guru. We can imagine that these thoughts are not ours. To fill the mind with positive thoughts, we can listen to or read stories of God, chant our mantra incessantly, do our spiritual practices regularly, and do good deeds. When the mind becomes purified, we will rise to superhuman planes and become divine. As the churning continued, many precious things surfaced from the sea of milk: *Airavat*, Goddess Lakshmi, *Dhanwantari*.... Finally, the urn containing the nectar of immortality surfaced. Likewise, those who continue their austerities until the end win the urn of ambrosia. Let us pray for divine blessings so that we can continue our spiritual journey fearlessly, undeterred by obstacles, and meet success.

28

The Magnificence of the Bhagavad Gita

The Mahabharata War happened in the outer world. But Lord Krishna's message in the *Bhagavad Gita* is a compendium of shortcuts to annihilate the inner foes. We cannot have peace without destroying the foes within. This is the solution to all problems in the outer world. It may be easy to win external wars but it is not as easy to emerge victorious on the inner battlefield. It is not as easy to combat our own likes and dislikes. We might mistake our negativities for near and dear ones. The story of Arjuna, who became despondent at the sight of his relatives and became reluctant to fight, is the story of each one of us who shies away from confronting our own negativities.

Through the *Gita*, the Lord strives to unveil the secrets of becoming invincible. The *Gita* is a dialogue between man and God. Who am I? Who is God? Why this universe? Why life? Does life end on death? What happens after death? Are there means to be happy in life and in the afterlife? The Lord provides clear answers to these and many more such queries in the *Gita*. Perhaps no other book propounds such profound principles as the *Gita*.

An Arab asked Amma, "Why is this science not included in the Indian educational curriculum?" A member of a royal family, he paid Amma a secret visit when She visited Reunion Island for programmes. Family feuds had dragged him to the brink of suicide. It was then that Murali Menon, his friend, gave him an English translation of the *Gita*. He took to reading it daily. Soon, his suicidal thoughts disappeared. He regained the strength to steer his life ahead. He then asked his friend, "There was a Krishna in the *Dwapara Yuga* (the third of the four ages by ancient Indian cosmology). Could you name someone like Him who is a contemporary?"

Murali Menon had been a devotee of Amma for a long time, and he invited his Arab friend to meet Amma at Her Reunion Island programme. After having Amma's blessing, he observed, "I have regained my confidence and grasped the meaning of the *Gita!*"

The rishis who gave us the *Gita* had no caste or religion, only love. They regarded all human beings through eyes of love and prayed for the welfare of the world. Those venerable rishis had attained the necessary purity to hear God's voice within and dedicated their lives to the cause of the world. The secrets they revealed were not intended exclusively for adherents of any particular religion. There is only one God. Whoever knows Him attains His realm, and becomes one with Him. From time to time, He incarnates to remind humanity of the purpose of human life. An ordinary person strives day and night to raise a family. He soon tires helplessly and cannot please his family. Amma works indefatigably to make millions happy, demonstrating to the world what can happen if divine power is awakened. The world reveres mahatmas like Amma. Why grieve when nature is ever ready to open up new vistas of bliss and intuitive experience? In order to experience the truth that nothing in this world can make us sad, we must first realise our real potential.

Sanatana Dharma ('Eternal Law,' the life culture and knowledge system of Bharat) does not accept that man is a weakling or sinner. On the contrary, the rishis proclaimed that all are embodiments of the Supreme. The same divine effulgence resides in all beings. If God is omnipresent, there is no place in nature where He is not. Just as a spark can raze an entire forest, a little divine power is all that it takes to reduce the wilderness of woes to ash, and open up the wonder-world of bliss for us.

Whatever happens outside happens inside, too. Whatever happens inside becomes reflected outside. Inner purity makes life beautiful. Without it, life will be filled with conflict and strife. Our sages desired that no wars be waged in the world. All wars originate in human minds. Long before swords get smeared with blood, the flames of lust, wrath and passion would have begun to rage in the human mind. Our emotions within are eventually reflected in the external world. Through the *Gita*, the Lord reveals ways to end the inner turmoil and turbulence.

The dharma of a soldier is to guard his land. He does not fight out of personal hatred. When the enemy attacks, there is no time to consider who it was that attacked; the soldier must act at once or risk putting the lives of millions of people in danger. The atom bomb that was dropped in Hiroshima killed hundreds of thousands in an instant. Similarly, a thought that germinates in one person's mind can affect affects hundreds of thousands of people. Vyasa reminds us that it was an impure thought in the mind of a single person that led to the Mahabharata War. The message of the *Mahabharata* is to annihilate the Kaurava army within. That is what the *Gita* teaches.

Amma says that although people regard themselves as intellectual beings, most are, in fact, emotional beings. Therefore, whatever happens in the world affects the mind easily. Until we have known the changeless in the changing world, we can become easily distressed. The world as we experience it now is at the lowest level of the mind. As the mind evolves, the world will begin to appear different. The world that jnanis perceive is blissful and pervaded by divine effulgence.

Like a mother holding her child's hand as they walk, Amma is holding our hands and leading us to that elevated plane. To bring about a change in perspective and purify the mind, *sadhana* (spiritual practice) is necessary. Amma has prescribed spiritual practices for Her children. Let us practice them with regularity and steadfastness. We might not see mahatmas doing those practices; that is because they are already established in the state of Self-realization. *Avadhutas* (jnanis who do not conform to social norms) may act crazy but they enjoy inner bliss. Though they may not pay heed to the outer world, they continuously shower blessings on all. Their mere presence is a blessing. Likewise, while living in this world, we should strive to change our mind. This is possible only through sadhana.

Sadhana confers what external objects can never give. We will begin to see what cannot be seen with our physical eyes. We will be able to grasp many things that are inaccessible to the senses. We will soon see that there is a realm of intuitive bliss.

At present, our focus is on external affairs: make money, gain an elevated social position; be extolled by others. If we achieve these goals, we think we will be happy. Of course, we might be able to gain all these. Wealth comes, but it goes, too. People may praise but they can also condemn. Positions will come and go. We may smile in happiness; we may also cry in grief. This is the experience of one who relies on the external world.

For one whose focus is on cultivating the inner life, external losses will not matter much. From the heights, we can see the mortality of things below. However, it is difficult know about the peaks of immortality from the valleys of mortality. To rise to such heights, Amma says that we must dissolve the mind. Even in ordinary life, we have experienced how we will fail to notice something if we are engrossed in something else. If we can cultivate a mother's love for her child, the millionaire's love for money, and the sensualist's love for pleasure, spiritual disciplines will become easy. If we wish to remain unaffected by the vicissitudes of life, we must become attuned to the inner world.

The following incident happened years before Amma's ashram took shape. During Devi Bhava, Amma took a tender coconut, sliced away its top, poured sacred ash into it, and gave the coconut to a woman, asking her to pour the contents on her son's head when she returned home. The woman wondered if she was supposed to pour the coconut water on his head or into his mouth. Why would anyone pour coconut water on the head?

The son used to come for Devi Bhava darshans regularly, and usually meditated beside Amma for hours on end. Perhaps Amma had wanted to give him the tender coconut as he was not there that evening; so surmised the woman.

Devi Bhava ended the next morning. On reaching home, she saw a crowd there. Her son was lying unconscious. She was told that he had been brought home unconscious from the temple the night before. The woman emptied the coconut water on her son's head. A little later, he opened his eyes. He told his mother than he had seen the form of Devi in the temple shrine, and must have fainted from fright.

How did Amma know all this, sitting 'far away'? Like Vishnu, Amma senses the pulsations of all sentient and insentient beings within Her.

All his life, man seeks peace and happiness. But when he looks for them in external objects, he cannot find them. Soon after electricity was discovered, a scientist installed electric lights in his house. When a friend visited, he was amazed when the lights came on. He looked around in wonderment. Later when he wanted to sleep, he found the light disturbing but did not know how to turn it off. Mounting a stool, he blew at the bulb, fanned it and tried other means, to no avail. As he was too embarrassed to ask the scientist, he spent the whole night tossing and turning.

The next morning, the scientist asked him, "Did you sleep well?"

The guest said, "I could not sleep at all! I was trying to put out the light the whole night but failed."

The scientist said, "Oh, it's very simple. See the switch here? Press it and the light goes out!"

"How simple it is. If only I had asked you last night, I could have slept well!" the guest said. He could have asked earlier but his pride did not permit him.

Likewise, we can switch off the miseries of life. We must learn to switch off the mind. Good actions are those performed with good intentions. Good actions are worship. For students, studying wholeheartedly is part of worship.

Once, there was a child with an ugly hunch on his back. People would laugh or scoff on seeing him, and this hurt him a lot. He even feared going out. One day, when he went out, he saw some people looking sad. He asked them, "Why are you so sad?" He then learnt that a thief had burgled their home and taken away all their belongings. As he did not know how to help, the hunchback left them. As he was walking away, he heard laughter. Turning around, he saw that the people who had been upset by the theft were laughing at the sight of his hunch. He thought, if people can laugh because of him, what a blessing his life is. From that day onwards, he took to mingling with people. By helping countless grief-stricken people laugh, he earned a lot of spiritual merit.

Long ago, when Sage Ashtavakra walked into the court of King Janaka, the scholars assembled there started laughing. Ashtavakra was twisted in eight different parts of his body; hence the name Ashtavakra, which literally means 'eight twists.' Seeing him walk had evoked laughter. Seeing them laugh, Ashtavakra also started laughing. But only King Janaka, who was Self-realized, understood the meaning of Ashtavakra's laughter. To teach the others a lesson, the king asked Ashtavakra, "Why are you laughing?"

The sage said, "These people are laughing at my physical deformity. Though they are scholars, they can see only the external. How then can they contemplate spiritual matters? Thinking thus, I couldn't help laughing."

Everything in this world is divine. Modern science states that everything is energy, and that there is nothing inert. Everything in nature understands love. That is why Amma tells us not to condemn anything. We must cultivate reverence for everything as God dwells in everything. We may first regard ourselves with respect, seeing the body as a temple. We should not debase this shrine. Similarly, we must also revere others. Only one who respects himself can respect others. We must first appreciate our own virtues, and then see virtues in others. One who strives to see goodness in others comes to experience that God is present everywhere in nature. Such a person enjoys the protection of all that is sentient and insentient in it.

Living in this world, we enjoy many things for free: sunlight, air, etc. We do not give anything in return for these. Many defile nature with negative thoughts, but not many try purify it through prayer. A selfish person can never find happiness in the world. Only selfless people can enjoy life. The mother is the first university. Education begins in the mother's womb. The mother's thoughts create the infant's mind. Therefore, in the olden days, pregnant women would spend time contemplating God. In order to have a virtuous and good-natured child, a mother would observe austerities.

Today, even mothers are blind to the fact that whatever they see becomes imprinted on the children's minds. The mother's diet and thoughts influence the child's mind. So, the child has already received its first lesson even before it comes into the world. Once the child is born, it observes and learns many things from its father and mother. Thus, even before it starts going to school, half its education is over.

Dronacharya and Ekalavya

Dronacharya refused to teach Ekalavya archery, not because the latter was of low social status. A flaming torch shall not be given to a child. The forest dweller is innocent like a child. He could be naïve and lacking in discrimination. Imparting information to one who does not know how to use it could be dangerous. As a forest dweller, Ekalavya's duty was not the protection of his country. That is why Dronacharya did not accept him as disciple. Yet, Ekalavya won him over by his pure love and devotion. All the knowledge of the Guru welled up in his innocent heart. Such is the power of love. May Amma bless us with such love and devotion.

29

Bathing in the Ganges of Immortality

A human birth carries infinite potential. Life is an opportunity to gain perfection. The conscious or unconscious actions we perform in life are, in fact, directed towards achieving this perfection. We have a sense of shortcoming lurking within. We strive lifelong to resolve this sense. Yet, man discovers that the more he strives to eliminate his shortcomings, the more new ones emerge in quick succession. Thus, right from birth, man is preoccupied with remedying his sense of incompleteness. In infancy, he engages in play in order to compensate for the lack of fulfilment. Later, he believes that education can remove imperfection. Still later, he thinks that a job is the solution to his problem. After that, he imagines that he can find fulfilment in marriage. And then he hopes to derive satisfaction in children. Thus, his efforts to find fulfilment continue throughout his life. Yet he dies eventually, unable to find perfection and satisfaction. Mahatmas like Amma teach us the secret to making each and every moment of life enjoyable.

Amma tells the following story. A chariot rolls down and stops before a beggar on the streets. Guards briskly whisk him away. Bewildered, the poor man asks, "Why are you dragging me, an innocent man, away like this?" The guards say nothing. The chariot goes straight to the palace. Thousands of people are waiting there to receive him. They welcome him cordially and usher him into the palace. Servants take him away to a bathroom, bathe him in warm water, and dress him in royal attire. Taken aback by all this, he asks, "Won't someone please tell me, what's all this about? No one says anything. They take him before the king, who places a crown on the beggar's head and proclaims, "This man is my chosen heir. From today onwards, he shall be your king!" The poor beggar does not understand anything. The erstwhile king reminds him, "You are my long-lost son!" The prince had gone missing from the palace during a war. The aging king sent agents far and wide to locate him. He had told them about certain signs on his son's person. They had discovered those tokens of recognition on the beggar. That was how the beggar came to be king!

The new king began to enjoy all the comforts and privileges of the royal life. After some time, he was seized by a strange desire: "What would it be like if I cast away my royal attire for a while, wear the tattered garments of a beggar, and roam the very streets where I used to beg for so long?"

So he sauntered along the same old streets in the guise of a beggar. But there was a difference now. Walking the streets now was not at all like how it had been. Then, when someone tossed him a coin, his heart would leap for joy. When people slammed doors on him, swore at him, pelted stones at him or humiliate him in some way, he would cry in pain. But now, the coins he received did not give him any special happiness, for he did not consider them precious. After all, he was custodian of priceless wealth. When people slammed their doors or swore at him, it only made him smile. "Poor people! They don't know who I am," he said to himself. He felt no hate towards them. The king in the guise of a beggar relished every bit of the drama. Mahatmas like Amma live in this world like the king. They live in a human guise, knowing fully well that they are God. Such are the Avatars.

The word 'avatar' means descent; God's descent from the divine abode to the plane of human beings. Amma says that, in reality, each of us is an avatar. We are jeevatmas descended from the state of the Paramatma. When we gain this knowledge, all sorrows will vanish. Every moment of life will become blissful. Nothing else we gain in life will satisfy us. Our role in life is meant to help us attain the bliss of God-realization. Those who enact each scene to perfection qualify for attaining the Supreme! The mahatmas who live among us are qualified to help us in this.

Amma did not choose to hide Herself in some cave to enjoy happiness for Herself. Such mahatmas—all Avatars—take on the pains of the world. What they offer in return is a life of self-sacrifice.

If we understand the greatness of human life, we will neither buckle under the pressure of life's minor sorrows nor exult in its minor pleasures. When pleasures come, we must try to keep our ego at bay while rejoicing. When sorrows come, we must consider it an opportunity to call upon God. Both pains and pleasures are occasions to reach Him. Pure minds can make this world even more beautiful than the worlds of the gods. To gain this purity, sadhana is necessary. Even though worldly things are necessary for us to live our lives in the world, it is spiritual experience alone that truly fulfils. Mahatmas show us how we can attain the state of God while alive.

In north Kerala, there is ritual form of worship known as *theyyams*. The players become transformed into gods during the theyyams, thus becoming worthy of worship. They even become powerful enough to bless others. The players shed their ordinary form and nature, and manifest divine power. We can transform everything with our mental resolve. There are many ritualistic art forms in Kerala that clearly demonstrate that a pure resolve is all one needs to rise from the lowest levels of the mind to exalted realms. We experience the world of pleasures and sorrows at the mind's lowest level. There are many ways to raise the mind to higher levels. When we have transcended all these levels and arrive at the state beyond the mind and intellect, we experience perfection. These ritualistic art forms can give us a taste of this experience, at least temporarily. Such art forms prove that even an ordinary human possesses divine power. However, to access this wholesome experience, one must follow a strict regimen according to certain protocols to bring about the necessary inner purity.

Another ritual is the *agnikkavadi*, a ritualistic fire dance. Hundreds of people bearing *kavadis* (arched-shaped structures carried on shoulders) arrive in a procession at a Lord Muruga temple. Huge crowds congregate there to witness their walking on fiery coals. The devotees, including children and elderly grown-ups, carry the kavadis and walk slowly and fearlessly over sizzling embers. Only the man standing in the front and giving instructions runs. All the others walk leisurely, for they have no body consciousness.

As they walk in a trance over fire, an ecstatic mood is created by the *chenda* beats and the celebrative yelling. This ritual is proof that we can rise from the earthy dimension (*prithvi*) that connects us to the gross earth, through *jala* (water), *agni* (fire), *vayu* (air) and *akasa* (space), whenever the mind disappears. When the mind ceases to exist, we transcend the laws of the *panchabhutas*, the five physical elements of creation. The panchabhutas yield to us. In meditation, a yogi can experience these realms. There are countless unclad yogis performing intense *tapas* (spiritual austerities) in the sub-zero temperatures of Himalayan regions. They can wilfully regulate their body temperatures. Our body is actually a storehouse of such wonders. We know only the lowest rung of the body. Art forms, yajnas, pujas and prayers are necessary to awaken the divine aspects within so as to tap into our hidden potentials. That is why the rishis did not separate or compartmentalise material life and spirituality.

The rishis gave us rituals and art forms so that we can rise above the confines of the body, mind and intellect, make every moment of our life blissful, and attain to the lofty realms of spirituality. They were not superstitions but means to lead us beyond physicality. All worship, prayers and rituals are means to this end. God has no use for them. They exist only to awaken the divinity latent in us.

The Guru is God come in the form of a human being to guide seekers. It is God's grace that assumes the form of the Guru. To see the Guru is to see God Itself. The Guru is one with God. The Guru awakens devotion in us. The Guru's presence purifies all. Amma is the ocean of bliss, knowledge and compassion. She is capable of eradicating all sorrows and obstacles. When Amma hugs us, our *bhava roga* (disease of worldliness) is being healed. She can elevate us to the supreme state of Godhood. May Amma bless us all that we overcome all limitations and bathe in the waters of the Amrita-ganga, the Ganges of Immortality, and attain God-realisation.

30

"Amma is with You"

In a torrential outpour of unchecked maternal love, a sweet smile playing on Her lips, Amma embraces us and whispers in our ears, "Children, Amma is with you!"

Thereafter, we realize throughout our life that those words are not hollow. When we are healthy, wealthy and powerful, many people will be drawn to us. But when we are suffering, no one will care to give us company. Only late in life do we realise that we are utterly alone in the battlefield of life. Our own body might not even obey us. It is not easy to win this battle all alone. It is then that Amma's comforting words can motivate us.

Our Guru will always be there with us, through good and bad times alike, and even after our death. The merit we have earned over lifetimes has brought us to a Sadguru like Amma.

It is impossible for our tiny intellect to comprehend the nameless, formless omnipresent God. There are no shortcuts to knowing this effulgence, immanent in creation. God cannot be known through our senses, which are limited.

Yet, difficult as it may be to know the Supreme, the sages of yore devised methods by which we can. They declare that it is possible to know God by observing certain disciplines in life.

You cannot look up at the blazing sun with naked eyes. Even if you did, you would not be able to see it properly. You will also cause damage to your eyes. As our naked eyes are not powerful enough to withstand the brilliance of the sunlight, the Guru appears like the moon that transforms the dazzling rays of the sun into soft and cool radiance.

As most of us are incapable of apprehending the all-pervading God, cosmic consciousness incarnates as a Guru, embodying all the divine qualities and attributes. The help of a Sadguru is necessary to know and experience God.

184

We might have several teachers in our life. All those who teach us good things are our teachers. Each and every object in the universe can be our teacher at different times. We may even have to learn from our own body. The present form and beauty of the body are not going to last forever. We usually realize this only late in life. Therefore, we must try to realize the immortal effulgence dwelling in the body while we are still alive. In order

to experience the effulgent self, the eye of knowledge needs to open. Only the Guru's blessings can help us remove the cataract of ignorance.

That is why the rishis prayed, "I take refuge in the three-eyed Supreme Lord (Lord Siva). There is no redemption from worldly sorrows and the cycle of birth and death unless the eye of intuition opens." It is the Guru who redeems us from this world. He appears before us in physical form, like the tender moonlight of knowledge, awakens the Guru within us, and bestows on us the experience of the inner effulgence.

Just as water vapour pervades the atmosphere, God's effulgence pervades the whole of creation. If water vapour were condensed, it would become fresh and pure water, pouring from the heights to the lower regions, and assuming the shape of the container that collects it.

Nothing is impossible for the omnipotent God. If He were one incapable of taking a form, how could He be all powerful? Though He exceeds names and forms, He can become anything because He is all powerful. Believers usually adopt a form to their liking and worship it. Eventually, they are blessed with the darshan of their ishta-murti (personal god). God can assume as many forms as there are human temperaments. These forms are what we call ishtadeva or ishtadevata. The sound vibrations that the rishis heard when they had visions of God became mantras. Those who recited those mantras were blessed with the darshan of those deities. In order to obtain the darshan of the personal god, an attitude of self-sacrifice and devotion is necessary.

Condensed vapour becomes flowing water, which when solidified by the chill becomes snow, which has perceptible shapes. Likewise, the formless incarnates on earth to guide ordinary people towards God. Just like a magician choosing to reveal his secrets, God unveils His maya and strives to impart the understanding of the mysteries of creation. Once we learn these secrets, life becomes a playground. First, we must cleanse the mind of its negativities and be ready to listen to the Guru's instructions.

Often, it is amid critical times that instruction becomes effective. The Guru waits patiently for the opportune moment, like a mother who waits patiently for her child to call out to her after he has become fatigued by playing and feels hungry. Similarly, the Guru, who is an embodiment of self-sacrifice, patiently waits to receive all our sorrows and to shoulder the burden of our ignorance.

The Universal Mother's love and compassion know no limits. She lives among us as Amritavarshini, Bestower of Ambrosia. We have only our pains and negativity to offer Her. In return, She showers divine love on us. Amma does not look at whether or not we are deserving. If we are undeserving, Amma teaches us how we can become deserving. We might not be *uttamadhikaris* (the highest grade of seekers). Nevertheless, Amma continues with the process of cleansing us of our negativities, and eventually transforms us into embodiments of innocence.

Amma says, "Children, in order to scale the heights, your legs alone aren't enough. You must also use our wings. Spread your wings and take off! Leaving the boundaries behind, rise up from the realms of body, mind and intellect, and enjoy the bliss of eternal freedom. Fear not. Amma is with you."